West Vancouver
- West Bay
- MATHERS AV
- 99
- INGLEWOOD AV
- Park Royal
- MARINE DR
- TAYLOR WAY
- 14
- Suspension Bridge & Park
- QUEENS RD
- MARINE DR
- 18
- North Vancouver
- Ambleside Park
- LIONS GATE BR.
- First Narrows
- CAPILANO 5 I.R.
- WELCH ST
- MISSION I.R.
- 3RD ST
- Prospect Pt.
- Stanley Park
- Ferguson Pt.
- 1A 99
- Vancouver Aquarium & Zoo
- Burrard
- Sea Bus
- Canada Place
- Vancouver Harbour
- Burrard Inlet
- GEORGIA ST
- English Bay
- Old Hastings Mill Store
- Vancouver Maritime Museum
- Vanier Park
- DAVIE ST
- West End
- BURRARD ST
- Gastown
- HASTINGS ST
- Chinatown
- TELUS World
- Jericho Beach Park
- MARINE DR
- 4TH AV
- ALMA ST
- MACDONALD ST
- Vancouver Museum
- B.C. Place Stad.
- Rogers Arena
- CNR/VIA Station
- 7
- 8TH AV
- BLANCA ST
- BLVD
- Granville Island
- 12TH AV
- C.H.
- Hen
- 16TH AV
- Pacific Spirit Regional Park
- CROWN ST
- DUNBAR ST
- BLENHEIM ST
- MACKENZIE ST
- 33RD
- ARBUTUS ST
- AV
- OAK ST
- 99
- Vancouver
- Queen Elizabeth Park
- 33RD AV
- 12 99
- MARINE DR
- 41ST AV
- VanDusen Bot. Gdn.
- MAIN ST
- 41ST AV
- MUSQUEAM 2 I.R.
- Oakridge Centre
- 49TH
- GRANVILLE ST
- CAMBIE ST
- ONTARIO ST
- FRASER ST
- KNIGHT ST
- 49TH AV
- North Arm
- 57TH AV
- 57TH AV
- S.E. Ma
- Iona I.
- ch rk
- FERGUSON RD
- Sea Island
- 70TH AV
- Mitchell I.
- Vancouver International Airport (YVR)
- GRAUER RD
- GRANT MC CONACHIE WAY
- S.W. MARINE DR
- 99
- BRIDGEPORT RD
- North
- Middle Arm

VANCOUVER
COCKTAILS

AN ELEGANT COLLECTION OF OVER 100 RECIPES INSPIRED BY THE CITY ON THE SEA

JANET GYENES

CIDER MILL
PRESS

BOOK
PUBLISHERS

VANCOUVER COCKTAILS

ISBN-13: 978-1-64643-418-3
ISBN-10: 1-64643-418-8

This book may be ordered by mail from the publisher. Please include $5.99 for postage and handling. Please support your local bookseller first!

Books published by Cider Mill Press Book Publishers are available at special discounts for bulk purchases in the United States by corporations, institutions, and other organizations. For more information, please contact the publisher.

Cider Mill Press Book Publishers
"Where good books are ready for press"
501 Nelson Place
Nashville, Tennessee 37214
cidermillpress.com

Typography: Dazzle, Avenir, Copperplate, Sackers, Warnock

Photography credits on page 362

Printed in India

23 24 25 26 27 REP 5 4 3 2 1

First Edition

CONTENTS

INTRODUCTION

"Vancouver is an antithesis looking for its synthesis;
it is a city with a split personality."
—Daniel Francis, *Becoming Vancouver: A History*

Vancouver is a shape-shifter. A youthful charmer always changing its mind about what it wants to be and who its heroes are. Spread along the sea and scrambling up craggy mountains crowned by conifers, its horizons lost in mercurial skies, the city of 662,000 (2.65 million in Metro Vancouver) draws comparisons to Seattle. Or San Francisco—the Golden Gate Bridge is strikingly similar to our Lions Gate, a forest-green beauty built for the Guinness family. With its densely populated downtown core punctuated by a forest of steel, Vancouver is often envisioned as a slightly less cyberpunk stand-in for Hong Kong. Add sobriquets such as Hollywood North and "Vansterdam" to the mix and its chameleonic nature becomes clear. And when more than 43,000 cherry trees rain pink on the city streets in spring, that creates more comparisons, more confusion, as to who this city belongs to and how it became what it is.

"On one hand it is a 'world-class city' striving for a size and a sophistication that might rank it on a par with any of the great metropolises of the world," says author Daniel Francis. "On the other hand, it is a 'liveable city' maintaining a slower lifestyle and keeping development to a human scale while making the most of its privileged natural assets. This tension plays out in almost every aspect of urban life."

Call it angst—or emergence. Vancouver is a city still growing into itself, beauty and blemishes alike. It's a place where sandy beaches and ragged shorelines encircle urban areas. Diverse neighborhoods have morphed into living art exhibits composed of outsize sculptures and multistory murals that invite conversation and contemplation. A world of cuisines and cocktails defies definition or categorization yet embodies the essence of what Vancouver is now and a vision of what it will become.

VANCOUVER'S COCKTAIL SCENE

The cocktail scene is evolving from drinking and dining to engaging in an experience engineered to create a sense of place. While Vancouver's best bartenders will always have one eye on the world's cocktail scene, they're increasingly looking inward. And, after witnessing the city's bartenders compete against thousands and consistently take top prizes on a global stage, outsiders are now training their attention on Vancouver. Mentorship is massive here and the bartender community is close-knit and eager to support each other's rising stars.

World champions from Vancouver who are still bringing their skills to the city's greatest bars and restaurants include Sabrine Dhaliwal (Chickadee Room) Grant Sceney (Fairmont Lobby Lounge and RawBar), Jeff Savage (Botanist Bar), Dylan Riches (Published On Main), Max Curzon-Price (SUYO), Alex Black (Laowai, Bagheera) and others who have shared recipes in *Vancouver Cocktails*. Others still, such as international award winners David Wolowidnyk (Bombay Sapphire: World's Most Imaginative Bartender), Lauren Mote (World Class Canada in 2015) and Kaitlyn Stewart (World's #1 Bartender at the World Class Bartender of the Year Competition 2017), are plying their craft while taking on roles as mentors, creators, and ambassadors for global brands.

They, too, are shape-shifters, moving among establishments that have been recognized and ranked by organizations such as Canada's 100 Best, Michelin, Tales of the Cocktail, Top 500 Bars, and others, elevating the industry to new heights. Wherever you decide to drink in Vancouver, whether it's a Michelin-starred restaurant, a speakeasy, or a distillery lounge, there will always be a good seat at the bar.

Alannah Taylor, bartender at Capo and the Spritz. See her cocktail creations on pages 92–95 and 328–31.

Workers at Hastings Saw Mill, 1925. Photograph by Leonard Frank and maintained by Vancouver Public Library.

UNFOLDING VANCOUVER

"In the beginning, there was booze."

Douglas L. Hamilton writes this plainly in his book *Sobering Dilemma: A History of Prohibition in British Columbia.* "Long before humans trod the planet, fruits ripened, rotted and fermented, producing ethyl alcohol. . . . Of all the intoxicants used in the world today, alcohol has been around the longest," he writes. "Human fondness for drink predates the use of cannabis, opium, coca, tea and coffee."

The history of distilling goes back thousands of years. Yet it's impossible to separate the virtues and vices of alcohol from politics, power, morality, and money. All those elements helped shape a story that started in a tiny outpost more than 150 years ago when the first European settlers arrived on the unceded territories of the xwməθkwəy'əm

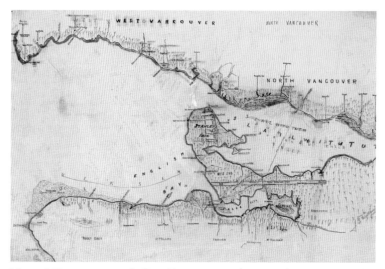

Map of Vancouver era before European settlement, drawn in 1932 by Major James Skitt Matthews and maintained by the City of Vancouver Archives.

(Musqueam), Skwxwú7mesh (Squamish), and səlilwətaɬ (Tsleil-Wau-tuth) Nations—the city of Vancouver as we know it today. This place, though, is still their ancestral territory, which they have stewarded since time immemorial.

Twenty-four hours. By all accounts, that's how long it took for thirsty workers from the Hastings Mill to team up one day in 1867 and slap together a saloon near a grove of maple trees in an industrial backwater, which wouldn't become a bona fide city until almost two decades later. But what payoff precipitated this rush job in the first place? One that yielded a board-and-batten shack measuring 12 by 24 feet called the Globe Saloon? It was the command of Captain John Deighton who, in turn, promised the sawmill workers all the whiskey they could drink if they just built him a bar.

Fishing on Vancouver Island, 1936

THE RISE OF GASTOWN

Originally from Hull, England, where he worked on ships, Deighton decamped to the United States, piloting boats in New York and San Francisco. When word got out in 1858 that gold had been discovered on the Fraser River, an estimated 25,000 to 40,000 fortune-seekers (largely from California) flooded north to the two British colonies: Vancouver Island and British Columbia (BC). Deighton was one of them.

"For the settlers of the few towns in the twin colonies, the streets seemed full of drunken rowdies, shady gamblers, thieving camp followers and prostitutes of every colour," writes Hamilton. In 1858, the British Columbia Constabulary was established to help curb the chaos. The temperance organizations soon followed, flooding the country from sea to sea. Hamilton, the Prohibition scholar, reveals another historic event that's little known or at least hardly written about. From 1884 to 1985 (that's not a typo), it was illegal for Indigenous people to buy or consume alcohol. Anyone convicted would be fined 100 pounds.

"Before the arrival of Europeans in the late 18th century," Hamilton writes, "alcoholic beverages were unknown in present-day British Columbia." European traders first arrived on the north coast of BC, exchanging liquor and guns with Indigenous people for sea otter pelts. At the turn of the century, American traders took over when the sea otter population declined. They continued a similar trading practice of bartering with booze. Hamilton says the first prohibition in the 1800s and the one that would come decades later were based on three things: race, class, and place.

It's hard to know if Deighton stuck to the laws. He left the coast again to join in the Cariboo Gold Rush, in BC's interior, but had little luck. Deighton then settled in New Westminster in 1862, which was the capital of colonial British Columbia until 1866 (the two colonies merged, and Victoria became the capital). It was in New Westminster that Deighton acquired the first Globe Saloon, as well as the nickname "Gassy Jack," for regaling his guests with yarns from his adventures.

A handwritten account by Major James Skitt Matthews (1878–1970), the City of Vancouver's first archivist, vividly describes Deighton: "He was a man of broad, ready humor, spicy, crisp and ever-flowing, of grotesque Falstaffian dimensions, with a green, muddy, deep purple complexion that told its own story. He had the gift of grouping words, which he flung from him with the volubility of a fake doctor." Later down the page, Matthews added: "His invective on the Indian population was scathing, adjectives and similes heaped together, but all unprintable."

Deighton hadn't found success as a gold-rusher, boat pilot on the Fraser River, or saloon-keeper. In fact, he was bankrupted after foolishly leaving the Globe in the hands of an American who decided to celebrate the 4th of July by raiding the till to purchase fireworks and letting guests drink for free. That's when Deighton, his Indigenous wife, and her cousin and mother set off in a dugout canoe, arriving on the shore of what's now known as Burrard Inlet—with a dozen barrels of whiskey. Or so historians speculate.

They landed at the site of the sawmilling settlement and set up Globe 2.0. Hastings Mill was a company town—and dry. Until Deighton arrived, the mill workers would have had to make their way to New Westminster for a drink. The area was largely wilderness, but it was by no means uninhabited. The map on page 11 shows several communities scattered along the water and in the area that became Stanley Park. (When the first road around the park was built between 1887 and 1888, crews uncovered evidence of Indigenous inhabitation including human burial sites.)

Other buildings started to spring up around Deighton's drinking den, and the area took on the nickname of Gassy's Town, or Gastown,

Stanley Park Hotel, circa 1890. Photo by Major Matthews and maintained by the City of Vancouver Archives.

after its de facto founder. But the man better known as Gassy Jack, along with his enterprise, were shuffled along in 1870 when the now six-acre area was acknowledged as a townsite, and the surveyor's plan placed the squatter saloon in the middle of a street. Moreover, the fledgling Gastown was absorbed into the new site and named Granville for the British colonial secretary, Earl Granville.

No matter. The ever-enterprising Deighton purchased a lot next door for $135 and built the two-story Deighton Hotel, its verandah shaded by a maple tree, on the corner where Carrall and Water streets intersect. Deighton was held in esteem by the men who traded brawn for booze to build his saloon, but Major Matthews's blunt description sheds light on why "Gassy Jack" has been downgraded from hero to historical figure. After Deighton's wife died, he married her 12-year-old niece named Qua-hail-ya, or Madeline. The following year, in 1871, she gave birth to their child. (Major Matthews verified these details in later interviews with Qua-hail-ya. She died in her nineties.)

Granville Street circa 1902

The year 1871 was significant for the settlement that had sprung up around a saloon. Although the Dominion of Canada had formed in 1867, the colony of British Columbia was still a holdout. When the new nation finally offered some enticements, including a promise to build a national railway to link the west to the rest of Canada, the colony finally relented. On July 20, 1871, it officially became the sixth province to join the Confederation. Due to poor health, Deighton died in 1875 at the age of 44, having never found his fortune, and not being alive to see what Gastown would become.

THE RAILROAD ARRIVES, AND
TRAGEDY STRIKES

In the 1880s, the colossal task of building the Canadian Pacific Railway (CPR) required labor—and lots of it. Europeans were working on the eastern section, and at the same time, Chinese laborers were brought over from both California and China on ships to tackle the dangerous and tricky terrain on the western North American coast. "Two years before Vancouver was incorporated in April 1886, a count around Burrard Inlet had tallied 114 Chinese," writes Paul Yee in his book, *Saltwater City: Story of Vancouver's Chinese.* It provides vivid detail of

Buildings on Carrall Street boarded up in the wake of race riots in Vancouver's Chinatown, 1907. Photo by Philip Timms and maintained by Vancouver Public Library.

the hardscrabble and harrowing lives of some of the earliest immigrants to arrive in the area. Government records say that "by the end of 1882, of the 9,000 railway workers, 6,500 were Chinese Canadians."

With the CPR construction completed in 1885, Granville continued to expand. When the population had swelled to 1,000, the City of Vancouver was incorporated on April 6, 1886. The name Granville, of course, never stuck. This time, an American, William Van Horne, who was president of the Canadian Pacific Railway, introduced the idea of naming the city after British naval officer George Vancouver.

Less than three months later, on June 13, 1886, tragedy stuck. A brush fire raged through the wooden buildings, burning most of the new city down in as little as twenty minutes by some accounts. An article in the *New York Times* reported that some bar patrons, nonplussed by the new city going up in flames, simply kept drinking. Others saw an opportunity to loot bottles of liquor and kegs of beer.

Like most structures, the Deighton Hotel was a casualty of the fire. The maple tree is gone, too. In 1970, a bronze statue of "Gassy Jack" standing on a whiskey barrel was erected on the corner at Maple Tree Square, memorializing the spot where he'd opened the Globe. It's crucial to note that more than half a century later, in 2022, the statue was pulled down by protesters decrying Deighton as a symbol of colonialism and racism.

Progress didn't slow down after the fire. Just a month later, the first transcontinental train arrived in Port Moody, the westernmost point of the line, but with some money and favors trading hands, the CPR line was extended to where Gastown still sits today, earning Vancouver its new nickname: Terminal City. The drinking didn't stop, either. One case in point: On July 6, 1888, the SS *Beaver* (owned by the Hudson's Bay Company, which used her for maritime fur trading) ran aground near Stanley Park, hitting the rocks by Prospect Point. The Maritime Museum of British Columbia reveals the likely culprit: booze.

Of course, Major Mathews dutifully recorded the day's events. A pioneer said that "Captain Marchant was an 'old drunk' and the crew 'were all drunk the night the Beaver went on the rocks.'" Another person said the crew had set off without something essential: "They had forgotten the liquor—call it 'booze' if you want to—and they wanted (Marchant) to turn back to Vancouver so that they could get a supply. So he turned back, and in turning around he ran ashore."

Such behavior wasn't novel, especially since the new province's population was growing rapidly, doubling every decade, with thousands of men working in mining, fishing, logging, and building infrastructure. Because of the nature of the labor, few women were around, and the men were free of family responsibilities. Seasonal workers spent their leisure time drinking and carousing. Places where people could drink were always opening up. By 1893, the Vancouver Club welcomed an exclusive selection of members. The 1925 *About Town Cocktail Book*, which was rediscovered decades later, refers to recipes by Vancouver Club bar steward Joe Fitchett as well as classics such as the Bijou and Clover Club. It also includes some off-color quips and "wisdom": "A bootlegger is someone who knows enough to sell it but too much to drink it." Several blocks away, the Cambie Pub was established in 1897 and remains one of Vancouver's oldest and longest-running bars.

Every hotel had a watering hole, including the Alhambra Hotel, which occupied part of the new Byrnes Block that was built on the site of the former Deighton Hotel. The Victorian Italianate brick edifice is where beloved lifeguard Joe Fortes (see page 61) tended bar in 1898; it's one of the city's oldest buildings still standing. Saloons were allowed to operate twenty-four hours a day. Public drunkenness? Not a problem. Women working in red-light districts? They struck a symbiotic relationship with corrupt cops. Hamilton writes, "In Vancouver, notorious Dupont Street [East Pender] hosted 41 houses with 153 girls in 1906." Something else pivotal happened in 1906. On July 1 (Canada Day), liquor licensing laws changed, abolishing freestanding saloons, which required the city's bars to conform to the same rules as hotels. Naturally, the number of hotels built in the area rapidly increased. Another measure was enacted: the drinking age was raised from 16 to 18 (today it's 19).

BC had earned a reputation as being the Wild West. And things got worse, culminating in an anti-Asian riot that was initiated on September 7, 1907, when a mob stormed into Chinatown, smashing the windows of every building.

Cordover Street circa 1900

Vancouver had already expanded well beyond Gastown's brick buildings. Paul Yee writes that, by 1911, "Twenty-five years after incorporation, Saltwater City (a name Chinese newcomers gave to Vancouver) was home to 120,000 people; its Chinatown had grown from 100 people to 3,500 and from a few wooden shacks to several blocks of brick buildings. The streets and alleys were lined with stores of every kind that formed the new trading hub of Canada's Chinese. It was a community of established families and businesses that set down deep roots and cultivated lofty ambitions."

The CPR barons had lofty ambitions, too. They envisioned the city as a tourist destination and built grand railway hotels designed to entice and entertain travelers arriving by train. The CPR's 1888 Hotel Vancouver was the first of a trio it built bearing the same name, but the original was replaced by a more expansive and grander one in 1916. (It was demolished in 1949. The third Hotel Vancouver, built in 1939, still sits in the heart of downtown, as grand and as glam as ever.) By 1916, religious fervor had picked up and anti-alcohol, or temperance, groups united. Then, in 1917, women "who qualified as British subjects" got the right to vote in provincial elections, which upped the ante on the temperance movement. Finally, it happened: on October 1, 1917, Prohibition became law in BC.

HOTEL VANCOUVER & COURTHOUSE.

THE PROHIBITION ERA IN VANCOUVER

Naturally, the drinking didn't stop for long, if at all; it just went underground. In the years that followed, underground gambling, sex work, and opium and drinking dens, as well as bootlegging, proliferated. Hamilton, in *Sobering Dilemma*, writes, "In fact, the illicit booze trade was a small entrepreneur's dream. Unlike the traditional mining, logging and fishing industries, where a small minority at the very top took the lion's share of the profits, the bootlegger kept a much larger portion of the cash take." When the United States introduced its own Prohibition in 1920, a lucrative opportunity opened up in BC: rum running. Vancouver's seaside location made it easy to load fishing boats with booze that would be offloaded to larger vessels. Ships became floating liquor emporiums.

In short, Prohibition failed miserably. An article published by the Legislative Assembly of BC states, "The new law was difficult and expensive to enforce. Doctors freely prescribed liquor, bootleggers flourished, and bars started selling low-alcohol 'near beer.'" But the government only offered two options for citizens during a referendum on the booze ban: keep the existing legislation or opt for a new act that gave the government more control over the sale of legal alcohol.

On June 15, 1921, Prohibition in BC was officially repealed. That day, the first government liquor stores opened. And they're still operating throughout the province today. Customers flooded to the stores, paying their $5 annual permit after a "character check." And spirits were priced much higher than beer to encourage purchase of the lower-alcohol product. Hamilton writes, "Telling, an estimated 75 percent were American customers escaping their own prohibition."

Legal drinking had returned. After Prohibition was repealed, all unlicensed drinking was banned, writes Robert Campbell in *Demon Rum or Easy Money: Government Control of Liquor in British Colum-*

bia from Prohibition to Privatization. In 1925, the government licensed hotel beer parlors. The Lamplighter Pub, which still occupies the ground floor of the 1901 Dominion Hotel, received Vancouver's first pub license. Two years later, in 1927, Hotel Georgia welcomed guests and even created an eponymous cocktail; you can order an updated version from the on-site Hawksworth Bar & Cocktail Lounge (see pages 82, 163, 269, and 316).

Bootlegging continued, though. But there was no way the government would let cities return to the raucous saloons of yore, and the Liquor Control Board (LCB) tried to keep a tight rein over permits, sales, and licensing. Hamilton says, "The LCB turned into a huge money-making machine, with the help from American liquor tourists." And it offered preferential treatment, too. Campbell says that although there was nothing to prevent beer parlors from opening outside of hotels, the LCB had "developed an understanding with the hotels' association. As long as they obeyed strict regulations, the hotels enjoyed a near monopoly. For the next fifty years they dominated the business of licensed public drinking in British Columbia."

Most of the legal oddities endured for decades: "No stand-up bar was permitted; patrons sat at tables and were served by waiters. Neither food nor entertainment was allowed. At first women were banned, allegedly to curb prostitution, and were later confined to areas separated from single men. In short, the only thing one could do in a beer parlour was drink."

THE RETURN OF THE SALOON, AND THE EARLY COCKTAIL DAYS

By the time 1952 rolled around, people were ready to vote in favor of expanding public drinking. Not surprisingly, the temperance-movement women were against cocktail lounges, and only wanted wine lists to be given out on request if restaurants were to be licensed. Hotel and restaurant associations had their own agendas.

Finally, a new liquor bill was proposed in 1953, which created four more licenses (dining room, dining lounge, lounge license, and public house license, which was designed to end the hotel monopoly), tangling the red tape even more. Another rule was issued, which British Columbians of today will be familiar with: "In dining rooms and dining lounges liquor could be sold only to a person who was having a meal, but 'meal' was not defined. Beer parlours could now sell sandwiches, but the supper-hour recess also remained." Campbell adds, "After nearly forty years the most prominent symbol of the saloon had returned to British Columbia. A generation before, beer by the glass had been rejected by a majority of the voters, who feared the return of the saloon and its stand-up bar and evil enticements."

The first cocktail lounge in Vancouver opened at the Sylvia Hotel in 1954, and it's been in operation ever since. In fact, some claim the once-forgotten Vancouver cocktail was invented in the Sylvia's medieval-themed "tilting" room. (But there's much more to that story; see page 40.) Over the decades, wrangling over liquor issues endured, but there have been a few gestures to loosen regulations. In 1988, the government ceded some of its monopoly, allowing private liquor stores to open, yet limiting the number of retail licenses. Distilleries have different hoops to jump through, whether commercial or craft (see Distillers + Makers, beginning on page 107). Regardless, the government still retains control of the sales of *all beverage alcohol* under the *Liquor Distribution Act.*

The complexity of liquor licenses created confusion for customers, too. Aside from liquor manufacturers, venues serving alcohol had to decide if they were a restaurant (food primarily) or a bar (liquor primarily). So if a patron went to a restaurant, they couldn't just cozy up in a booth and spend the day drinking; they also had to order food unless they were sitting in a separate lounge area.

That changed in 2015, when the *Liquor Control and Licensing Act* was overhauled, offering some new concessions like allowing licensees to participate in—yes—happy hour. Before then it was illegal to sell liquor at a discount. Every such step helps clear the confusion, but the government is still responsible for two contradicting goals: promoting moderation and generating revenue. Just as it has been since Prohibition was repealed more than a century ago.

NOTE ON RECIPES FOR COMPONENT INGREDIENTS

Making these recipes takes some time and commitment! But once you've done all the prep work for the components, the ingredients come together quickly for a crowd-pleasing cocktail. In cases where a high degree of precision is required, measurements have been provided in metric only.

Pourhouse's Espresso Manhattan (see page 71)

CLASSIC COCKTAILS

FITCHETT

VANCOUVER

VANCOUVER 2.0

OLD FASHIONED

FLAMING ROSEMARY GIMLET

CLASSIC NEGRONI

STRAWBERRY NEGRONI

NEGRONI SBAGLIATO

BOULEVARDIER

COBRA'S FANG

No surprise: the most celebrated classic cocktails weren't created in Canada. They were birthed in cities abroad such as Paris (French 75), London (Hanky Panky), and Venice (Aperol Spritz). And many influences migrated north of the 49th parallel from the United States, including New York (Manhattan), New Orleans (Sazerac), and San Francisco (Irish Coffee). Along with their geographic pedigrees, the ingredients in classic cocktails give us glimpses into the styles and times of when they originated. Learning about them can be as intoxicating as binge-watching a season of *Drunk History*. The stories are murky and contentious, with muddled facts and more versions than a Dirty Martini.

Some cocktails were originally crafted out of necessity—curatives like the Gin & Tonic (the slightly bitter mixer includes quinine, which wards off malaria) and the Gimlet (the lime was an antidote for scurvy). Often, other elements like bitters and sugar were added to mask the rank taste of cheap booze. And some "true" classics simply became impossible to make thanks to pests and politics.

A case in point: the Sazerac, which was (allegedly) first made with Cognac and absinthe in the 1880s. Not long after, rye replaced the grape-based spirit, possibly because of a sap-sucking insect called *phylloxera* that decimated Europe's vineyards. That was just the start of the Sazerac's evolution. In 1912, the United States banned an essential ingredient—absinthe—purportedly because it contained grand wormwood (*Artemisia absinthium*), which was thought to make people lose their minds (or an ear, if you were an absinthe aficionado like Van Gogh). Herbsaint, another anise-flavored liquor that didn't contain wormwood, was used instead. Absinthe was never illegal in Canada, but the ban in the United States lasted from 1912 until 2007. Traditionalists might maintain that no true Sazeracs were made (legally) in the States for a stretch of ninety-five years.

Another example of an original recipe requiring a remake is the Vesper. The cocktail became popularized after author Ian Fleming concocted the drink for suave spy James Bond in *Casino Royale*, published in 1953. The recipe, named for Bond girl Vesper Lind, called for Kina Lillet, which was discontinued in 1986 (the original was reformulated in 1985 to reduce the quantity of sugar and quinine to make it taste better). In 1958, Fleming created an enduring cocktail controversy when 007 requested his Martini be "shaken, not stirred"—considered a cocktail-making crime by many a mixologist.

Although these old tales are worth retelling, in a youngster of a city like Vancouver, classics aren't often menu mainstays. That's not to say local bartenders have forsaken the foundations of crafting a perfect Old Fashioned, Negroni, Gimlet (cue the controversy), or Martini (and again). It's just that classics are more likely to be front and center at upscale hotel lounges or sleek steakhouses, where timeless trumps trend.

Below are some faithful favorites everyone should mix up at least once—if not master—before messing with the formula. Like the city's Vancouver cocktail, whose backstory reads a bit like a spy novel where the hero just might be a bartender: this oddity stars the late actor Errol Flynn, playing himself, a devotee to the Vancouver cocktail when he visited the city in the 1950s.

DECODING THE "COCKTAIL"

"What is history but a fable agreed upon?"

The cocktail canon is a prime example of how time cements some stories and discredits others. For instance, the word "cocktail" is now believed to have first been printed on March 20, 1798, in London's *Morning Post and Gazetteer*. This discovery was only made in 2012 by cocktail historians Jared Brown and Anastatia Miller, who debunked the original belief that the word's first mention in print was in the April 28, 1803, issue of a newspaper called *The Farmer's Cabinet*: ". . . drank a glass of cocktail—excellent for the head . . ."

But the more provocative story is how the word came into the world in the first place. Frank Meier, acclaimed bartender at the Hôtel Ritz in Paris, wrote *The Artistry of Mixing Drinks*, which was published in 1936. His introduction describes how he found some old documents while researching his book, which tell a fantastic tale about a woman named Betsy Flanagan, who is credited with coining the term almost two decades earlier, around 1779.

It's a meandering story about a raucous event in Flanagan's tavern in Yorktown, Virginia, where she hosted American and French officers of the Revolutionary Army, serving them a beverage called a Bracer. (The 1895 book *Modern American Drinks* says the Bracer is a concoction of brandy, yellow Chartreuse, maraschino, absinthe, egg yolk, and fine sugar.) There was some flap about Flanagan promising to raid a nearby chicken coop kept by an Englishman she despised. Flanagan held true to her threat, one night serving the fowl to the officers for dinner and decorating bottles of Bracer with "cocks' tails." Meier wrote that the frequent orders and shouts of the night were, "Give us some more of those 'cocktails,'" and *"Vive la cocktail."*

He wouldn't vouch for the anecdote's authenticity (and Meier's own history is laced with conspiracy theories, as you'll later read) but he offers some sage advice:

The cocktail should always be perfect; there is no reason ever to drink a bad one. Almost any of the ingredients of which cocktails are composed might be better consumed 'straight' rather than just carelessly poured together.

And he ought to know. Meier created classics like the Bee's Knees (or not; read more on page 74) and the London Fog, which is not to be confused with the latte of the same name invented in Vancouver during the mid-1990s.

L'Abattoir bartender Rob Williams (see page 342)

FITCHETT

We've Been Making the 'Vancouver Cocktail' Wrong for 15 Years." That's the March 2, 2020, headline of an opinion piece written by award-winning bartender Alex Black for Scout, an online magazine dedicated to the city's food and culture. (Black is now cocktail director and managing partner at speakeasies Laowai Cocktail Bar, page 199, and Bagheera, page 282.)

The article traces local lore about where and when the city's namesake cocktail was first created (spoiler: not at the Sylvia Hotel in 1954, as once thought), complete with its strange-but-true revival in 2008, decades after the stirred drink had disappeared into obscurity.

TL;DR (but *do* look up Black's article): The mix of gin, Italian vermouth, Benedictine, and a dash of orange bitters that bartenders *thought* composed the Vancouver cocktail, well, wasn't correct. That recipe was for the Fitchett. Named for Joe Fitchett.

Misattribution and muddy details became clearer with a few clues, namely the rediscovery of the *About Town Cocktail Book*, published locally in 1925. Fitchett, who is credited with compiling the recipes, including the true Vancouver cocktail (made with French vermouth, minus the orange bitters, plus an olive) was the head bar steward at the Vancouver Club, which opened at its original location in 1893.

Leagh Barkley, director of the restaurant and bars at the Vancouver Club, confirms the Vancouver cocktail's origins, so it's possible that's where it was first sipped. Both recipes from the book are included below. Was it Joe Fitchett who invented it? It's still not clear. Regardless, if you're a guest at the Club, you can sip a Vancouver in the spot where it was likely created.

The Sylvia Hotel, which graces Beach Avenue with its iconic Boston ivy twisting up its brick façade, claims its then-named Tilting Room was Vancouver's first cocktail bar, opened in 1954. In Robert A. Campbell's book *Demon Rum or Easy Money*, he confirms the timing. The Sylvia's updated medieval-themed lounge bears touchstones from the past, and it's still a top-notch spot to drink and enjoy unspoiled views of English Bay.

Although a version of the Vancouver ("Sylvia's own") is listed front-and-center on the menu, noting it was a favorite of actor Errol Flynn, the ingredients listed are for the Fitchett. And despite rumors, the fifty-year-old Flynn didn't die at the Sylvia in 1959. An exhibit at the Vancouver Police Museum & Archives dispels the myth, stating he expired a few blocks away in the West End. Flynn had gone to an apartment at 1310 Burnaby Street to see the uncle of famed pianist Glenn Gould, who was a doctor. Complaining of back pain, Flynn went into a bedroom to rest, and later that evening, his seventeen-year-old "girlfriend" discovered him dead.

GLASSWARE: Coupe glass, chilled
GARNISH: Olive or cherry

- 50 percent gin
- 30 percent Italian vermouth
- 20 percent Benedictine
- Dash orange bitters

1. Combine all of the ingredients in a mixing glass with ice. Stir until chilled.

2. Strain the cocktail into the chilled coupe.

3. Garnish with an olive or cherry.

VANCOUVER

VANCOUVER CLUB, *ABOUT TOWN COCKTAIL BOOK*

GLASSWARE: Coupe glass, chilled

GARNISH: Olive

- 50 percent gin
- 30 percent French vermouth
- 20 percent Benedictine
- Dash orange bitters

1. Combine all of the ingredients in a mixing glass with ice. Stir until chilled.

2. Strain into the chilled coupe.

ST. REGIS

1-5 Lime Juice
1-5 Grenadine Syrup
3-5 Apple Jack

TUXEDO

WHEN you're all dressed up ready for dinner this Tuxedo special will set you off to a good start:

Half fill an ordinary-sized shaker with shaved ice
2 tablespoonfuls Sherry
½ wineglass Italian Vermouth
1 wineglass Gin

Shake well and strain into glasses.

VANCOUVER

Dash of Orange Bitters
50% Gin
30% French Vermouth
20% Benedictine
Olive

WILLIAMSON AND BARNEY

1 square inch of orange
1-3 of one lime
1 dessertspoonful of powdered Sugar

Mash well and add ½ whisky glassful of Bacardi Rum

WHISKY

1 teaspoonful Gum Syrup
2 dashes Angostura Bitters
1 teaspoonful Lemon Juice
1 cocktail glass Scotch Whisky
Cocktail shaker half filled with ice

Shake well, strain in cocktail glass and serve.

LOVE is like getting drunk, they say: Love is the liqueur, marriage the headache, and divorce the seidlitz.

VANCOUVER 2.0

NOTCH8 RESTAURANT & BAR, FAIRMONT HOTEL VANCOUVER, DOWNTOWN

Although it's rare to see the Vancouver cocktail (or the Fitchett, see page 38) on menus, Notch8 Restaurant & Bar offers a sophisticated solution to which version should prevail. The Vancouver 2.0. includes both sweet and dry vermouth and swaps out the Benedictine for B&B (a blend of 60 percent Benedictine and 40 percent French brandy).

Notch8 is a bit of a newcomer, but the glamorous railway-themed bar is situated in the lobby of the 1939 Fairmont Hotel Vancouver, instantly recognizable for its castle-like structure and mint-hued roof of oxidized copper. The downtown property plays a big role in Vancouver's history. When the Canadian Pacific Railway (CPR) built a line to connect the country from coast to coast in the 1880s, grand hotels, often designed to emulate French chateaux, provided respite for its well-heeled travelers. Train aficionados will know that Notch8 is the highest throttle position on a diesel locomotive. An elevated experience is what the bar aspires to with its offers of pre- and post-Prohibition cocktails.

◆

GLASSWARE: Coupe glass, chilled

GARNISH: Orange peel

- 1 oz. (30 ml) Long Table London Dry Gin
- 1 oz. (30 ml) B&B (see above)
- ½ oz. (15 ml) sweet vermouth
- ½ oz. (15 ml) dry vermouth

with cubed ice.

2. To chill, stir for 30 seconds, using a barspoon.

3. Strain the cocktail from the mixing beaker into the chilled coupe.

4. Garnish with the fresh orange peel.

THE ORIGINAL WHISKEY COCKTAIL

Whiskey, bitters, sugar, water. The Old Fashioned hasn't changed much since it was first conceived, straightforwardly embodying the definition of the word "cocktail" published in *The Balance and Columbian Repository* on May 13, 1806, as "a stimulating liquor, composed of spirts of any kind, sugar, water, and bitters." (World Cocktail Day is celebrated annually on May 13.)

If you consult old cocktail books like the 1895 *Modern American Drinks* (by George J. Kappeler), you'll find a trio of recipes that seem to define how the Old Fashioned found its formula. The Whiskey Cocktail includes, of course, whiskey and bitters (two dashes of Angostura or Peychaud's), plus two dashes of "gum-syrup." Kappeler's Old-Fashioned Whiskey Cocktail follows today's typical method: "Dissolve a small lump of sugar with a little water in a whiskey glass; add two dashes Angostura bitters, a small piece of ice, a piece of lemon peel, and one jigger of whiskey. He says to "Mix with a small barspoon and serve, leaving the spoon in the glass."

Kappeler also includes the prefix "old fashioned" on recipes that call for Holland gin, Tom gin, and brandy that follow the same steps. This led people (or just overthinking writers) to wonder if "old fashioned" was a method and the word "whiskey" was later dropped when it became the cocktail's de facto spirit. Fast forward to Harry Craddock's 1930 *The Savoy Cocktail Book* and you'll find the same recipe specifying "rye or Canadian Club whiskey." Craddock also includes a note that the cocktail can be made with "brandy, gin, rum, etc."

Whatever the origin or evolution (like the British Columbia Old Fashioned on page 174 made with breakfast-cereal-infused rye), the Old Fashioned is a prime example of how the whole should be much more than the sum of its parts. Each element complements the other, so all ingredients must be premium quality and measured precisely to transform simple to sublime.

OLD FASHIONED

HY'S STEAKHOUSE & COCKTAIL BAR, DOWNTOWN

Since 1962, Hy's Steakhouse & Cocktail Bar has been holding court on Hornby Street in Vancouver's financial district (the restaurant was established in Calgary in 1955). The classic steak house is on the ground floor, and at the top of a steep, brick-lined staircase is a drinking den wrapped in warm woods and where the menu includes dozens of whiskeys from across the globe. A few sips of a Macallan Fine Oak 30-year will set you back $300, but Hy's also offers an impressive selection of Canadian rye and BC craft whiskey.

One new release on the list, called Bearface Triple, comes from BC's Mark Anthony Group (the originators of White Claw, which debuted in the United States before Canadians could get their hands on the hard seltzer four years later). The single-grain Canadian whiskey uses a process called elemental aging, literally exposing the barreled spirit to the climes of Canada's extreme northern wilds. If that wasn't complicated enough, the whiskey is triple-aged: first for seven years in ex-bourbon American oak barrels, then in French oak red-wine casks and, finally, air-dried virgin Hungarian oak. It's just one example of the outsize creativity that BC distillers are bringing to palates both locally and globally.

With an Old Fashioned, there are so few ingredients and so little room to hide. Yet the stellar selection at Hy's opens the door to creativity and complexity. Its version of the venerable cocktail uses Jim Beam Black, an 86-proof bourbon aged in American white oak barrels for eight years, adding notes of smooth caramel and warm oak.

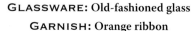

GLASSWARE: Old-fashioned glass

GARNISH: Orange ribbon

- 1 orange peel
- ½ oz. (15 ml) Demerara Syrup (see recipe below)

- 2 oz. (60 ml) Jim Beam Black
- 7 dashes Angostura bitters

1. Peel a large ribbon of orange rind. Release the essential oils by bruising the peel into a mixing glass with the syrup.

2. Add the bourbon, bitters, and ice.

3. Stir, counting to 10.

4. Strain the cocktail into an old-fashioned glass over new ice, preferably one large cube.

DEMERARA SYRUP: In a small pot, boil together equal parts demerara sugar and water until the sugar is fully dissolved. Allow it to cool. Pour the syrup into a clean, airtight container; store it in refrigerator. The syrup will last for one week.

A TIME FOR LIME

The Gimlet, for all intents and purposes, possibly altered the course of history by saving lives during long stretches at sea. It's high praise for a cocktail whose creation is often attributed to a surgeon—Rear-Admiral Sir Thomas Desmond Gimlette—and which was dosed in rations to sailors and officers in the British Royal Navy during the 19th century. Scurvy was the plague, lime juice was the cure, and the 114-proof gin (Navy strength) was used to wash the pure citrus down.

That simple and natural recipe was radically altered when Rose's Lime Juice, a concentrated cordial, was patented in 1867 by a lad named Lachlan Rose who hailed from Leith, Scotland. It offered a new way to preserve lime juice sans spirits (but with lots of sugar) that was then mixed in a 50:50 ratio with gin, eventually becoming the Gimlet go-to, even for polite British society.

In his 1930 tome, *The Savoy Cocktail Book*, famed English bartender Harry Craddock offers the Rose's 50:50 version (specifying stirring Burrough's Plymouth Gin with the cordial) plus a take called the Gimblet, which calls for one-quarter lime juice to three-quarters dry gin, shaken and strained, and topped with soda water.

The Gimlet enjoyed a mid-century revival with drinkers, thanks to Raymond Chandler's 1953 novel, *The Long Goodbye*. The author's hardboiled PI, Philip Marlowe, had a penchant for imbibing and opining. Sitting in a corner of the bar, Marlowe said: "They don't know how to make them here. . . . What they call a gimlet is just some lime or lemon juice and gin with a dash of sugar and bitters. A real gimlet is half gin and half Rose's Lime Juice and nothing else. It beats martinis hollow."

A TIME FOR BEES

Some 250,000 honeybees have called the Fairmont Waterfront Hotel's rooftop garden and apiary home since 2008. Along with more than 20 varieties of herbs, fruits, veggies, and edible blossoms, honey is harvested to make Fairmont Waterfront West Coast Wild Gin. (The unique gin is created in collaboration with Wayward Distillery on Vancouver Island, Canada's only distillery that uses up to 100 percent honey as a base for its gin and vodka.) It's crafted with fermented honey and traditionally harvested local botanicals including juniper, Nootka rose, bull kelp, spruce tips, cedar, and lavender. The complex and quintessentially local gin is mixed with equal parts lime juice and simple syrup—a brilliant take on the original.

FLAMING ROSEMARY GIMLET

ARC BAR, FAIRMONT WATERFRONT HOTEL, DOWNTOWN

At the ARC Bar in the Fairmont Waterfront Hotel, the Flaming Rosemary Gimlet isn't about staying true to history but focusing on a more sustainable future while celebrating Indigenous West Coast fauna. The gin and its krupnik liqueur make for one of ARC's "garden-to-class" cocktails.

◆

GLASSWARE: Old-fashioned glass*
GARNISH: Curled rosemary sprig

- 1½ oz. (45 ml) Fairmont Waterfront West Coast Wild Gin
- ¾ oz. (22.5 ml) fresh lime juice
- ¾ oz. (22.5 ml) simple syrup
- 1 large sprig fresh rosemary
- Green Chartreuse (in a mister)

1. In a pint mixing glass, add the gin, lime juice, and simple syrup.

2. Fill the glass with ice and shake vigorously. Set aside.

3. Curl the rosemary sprig in the bottom of an old-fashioned glass.*

4. Spritz the rosemary with green Chartreuse and ignite it with a lighter to toast the herbs. Let it sizzle for a few seconds, then strain the cocktail over the flaming rosemary.

5. Add fresh ice to fill.

*Be sure to use a tempered glass for this cocktail.

THE NEGRONI:
A TALE OF TWO COUNTS

Was the count who created the Negroni a Florentine who spent time in the States as a swashbuckling cowboy, rodeo clown, or "teacher of fencing" by the name of Camillo Negroni? Or was the cocktail first crafted by Pascale-Olivier Comte de Negroni, a Corsican general who dedicated forty-four years of his life to the French Army?

Has something been lost in translation? Or is this count conundrum a case of revisionist history?

It appears there might be more to the old chestnut about Count Camillo Negroni (the Italian) sidling up to bartender Fosco Scarselli in 1919 and asking for something more bracing in his Americano—a cocktail of Campari, sweet vermouth, and soda water. Scarselli is said to have replaced the soda with a shot of gin. *"Prego,"* we can imagine Negroni saying, happily taking credit for the now-classic concoction that has featured a 1:1:1 ratio of those three ingredients—Campari, sweet vermouth, and gin—ever since.

Now, if you know anything about Corsicans (hello, Napoléon), they're not ones to back down from a fight. In recent years, two family members of Pascale-Olivier Comte de Negroni have challenged that version of cocktail history, saying no such Count Camillo Negroni exists in their family lineage. Further, they offered proof in the form of a letter that revealed the French general had invented the eponymous cocktail in 1857 in Saint Louis, Senegal, where Pascale-Olivier was posted.

Plot twist: Campari was invented in 1860. As one writer suggests, perhaps we're pondering the wrong question. Not *who* created the Negroni, but *what* is the real cocktail? There are a number of prede- cessors from which the cocktail is said to have evolved. However, it wasn't until 1929 that the recipe as we know it—equal parts gin, Campari, and sweet vermouth—was written down, in the French book *L'heure du Cocktail*, written by Parisian bartenders Alimbau and Milhorat. Called a *Campari Mixte* ("Mixed Campari"), the cocktail is *bien mélanger* (shaken well) and served with lemon zest.

One account I read when researching the history conflated the Italian and French counts, creating a truly fantastical story where the tale of two count Negronis was (allegedly) one short. And perhaps the truth lies somewhere in the middle. Regardless, this is one classic whose history seems destined to keep developing.

I think the Negroni is the perfect cocktail because it is three liquors that I don't particularly like. I don't like Campari, and I don't like sweet vermouth and I don't particularly love gin. But you put them together with that little bit of orange rind in a perfect setting . . . It's just: It sets you up for dinner, in a way it makes you hungry, sands the edges off the afternoon. In an after dinner, it's settling. It is both aperitif and digestive. It's a rare drink that can do that.

—Anthony Bourdain

CLASSIC NEGRONI

FABLE KITCHEN, KITSILANO

When chef Trevor Bird competed in the famous "Restaurant Wars" episode of the TV series *Top Chef Canada*, his team's farm-to-table concept sparked the idea for a new restaurant's portmanteau: Fable. With a trio of locations in Vancouver's hottest neighborhoods (Kitsilano is where it originated), the restaurant was recently awarded Michelin's Bib Gourmand status. That well-earned accolade is rooted in the local and seasonal produce delivered daily to Fable from area farms, so it's no surprise that fresh berries make an appearance on the cocktail menu (along with locally distilled spirits).

Fable offers three takes on the Negroni. One is made with Sheringham Seaside Gin, distilled on Vancouver Island. It's infused with the expected botanicals like juniper and coriander, plus a hit of brine from local, sustainably harvested winged kelp. A less boozy choice is the TikTok-famous Negroni Sbagliato, where gin is substituted for Prosecco. For sustainable sipping, stir up the standout the Strawberry Negroni, which uses pesticide-free fruit from the McKim farm on Westham Island.

◆

GLASSWARE: Rocks glass
GARNISH: Orange peel

- 1 oz. (30 ml) Sheringham Seaside Gin
- 1 oz. (30 ml) Campari
- 1 oz. (30 ml) Cocchi Storico Vermouth di Torino

1. Add all of the ingredients to a mixing glass.

2. Add ice and stir until the mixing glass is very cold.

3. Single-strain the cocktail into a rocks glass over a king cube. Garnish with a creatively cut orange peel.

STRAWBERRY NEGRONI

FABLE KITCHEN, KITSILANO

Westham Island is a hidden farming treasure in the Lower Mainland and full of some of the most amazing fruits and vegetables you can get," says Kevin O'Neill, Fable Kitchen's general manager. "I wanted to incorporate produce from there into a cocktail and this bright tasty riff on the Negroni turned out beyond amazing. The red berry–forward Brockmans Gin, coupled with the fresh strawberry juice, is a match made in 'Westham Heaven.'"

GLASSWARE: Rocks glass
GARNISH: Dehydrated or fresh strawberry slice, cut vertically

- 1 oz. (30 ml) Brockmans Gin
- 1 oz. (30 ml) Campari
- 1 oz. (30 ml) Cinzano Rosso Vermouth
- ½ oz. (15 ml) Fresh Strawberry Juice (see recipe opposite)

1. Add the gin, Campari, vermouth, and strawberry juice to a mixing glass with ice.

2. Stir with a barspoon until the mixing glass is very chilled.

3. Single-strain the cocktail into a rocks glass over a king ice cube.

4. Garnish with the strawberry, placing it directly on top of the ice cube.

FRESH STRAWBERRY JUICE: Take fresh strawberries, wash and cut the tops off, then freeze them overnight. The next day, allow the strawberries to thaw at room temperature. Once thawed, place them in a Vitamix or high-powered blender and puree. Place a strainer lined with cheesecloth over a bowl. Pour the puree into the cheesecloth and lightly squeeze the juice to avoid strawberry pulp from coming through.

NEGRONI SBAGLIATO

FABLE KITCHEN, KITSILANO

T his cocktail sits somewhere between a Spritz and a Negroni in both bitterness and booziness," says Kevin O'Neill, general manager of Fable Kitchen. Sometimes social media can introduce us to things we never knew we wanted. The word *sbagliato* translates to "broken," but this Negroni riff is also of perfect illustration of a smart concept: drink your mistakes.

◆

GLASSWARE: Rocks glass

GARNISH: Orange peel

- 1 oz. (30 ml) Campari
- 1 oz. (30 ml) Carpano Antica Formula Vermouth
- 1½ oz. (45 ml) Rufino Prosecco, to top
- 1 barspoon green Chartreuse, to top

1. Pour the Campari and vermouth into a mixing glass.

2. Add ice and stir until the mixing glass is very cold.

3. Single-strain the cocktail into a rocks glass over a king cube. Top with Prosecco and finish with a barspoon of green Chartreuse.

4. Garnish with a creatively cut orange peel.

AN AMERICAN IN PARIS

This "cousin" of the Negroni, where gin is replaced with whiskey, was created in the 1920s by Erskine Gwynne, an American writer who decamped to Paris, where he founded the magazine *Boulevardier*.

Those with *un peu* French will know the word *boulevardier* describes a "man about town," as in someone who strolls Parisian boulevards. Today Gwynne might be called a "nepo baby," but in its January 7, 1929, issue, *Time* magazine referred to him as "the cherub-faced and rumpus-raising nephew" of General and Mrs. Cornelius Vanderbilt. His boozy beverage, obvs, made a better impression than he did.

Bartender Harry MacElhone (of that Harry's Bar, a Paris institution since 1911) is said to have handwritten Gwynne's recipe as a footnote in his 1927 book, *Barflies & Cocktails*, clearly attributing the Boulevardier to the writer. The book also carried a full-page ad for the magazine in its back pages, giving further credence to the pair's connection.

BOULEVARDIER

JOE FORTES SEAFOOD & CHOP HOUSE, DOWNTOWN

When you work at an institution like Joe Fortes, you don't forget your roots. And bartender Mark Paulhus shares his inspired Boulevardier recipe, "a big bold classic cocktail," he says. "It's strong yet friendly, like our namesake."

For more than thirty-five years, the restaurant (which features a wine room and intimate bar inside, and another bar at the back of the rooftop garden) has been a perennial favorite for aged steaks and freshly shucked oysters hauled out of BC's waters. It also memorializes its legendary namesake, Seraphim "Joe" Fortes, whose history is printed on the menus as a reminder that bighearted hospitality, like a classic cocktail, never goes out of style.

Fortes was likely born in Port of Spain, Trinidad and Tobago (with Barbadian roots), and became a competitive swimmer in Great Britain before immigrating to Canada one hundred years before the other Joe Fortes opened its doors in 1985. He was best known as Vancouver's first official lifeguard, and lived in a cottage at English Bay, where he spent summers teaching children to swim. (A marble drinking fountain in Alexandra Park across from the bay honors Fortes with a simple inscription: "Little children loved him.") Fortes also tended bar at the 1875 Sunnyside Hotel, in Maple

Tree Square. At the time, it was one of the oldest establishments in the Gastown neighborhood, when the city was still called Granville, but it was later destroyed in the Great Fire of 1886 when the newly incorporated city basically burned to the ground.

Paulhus honors the Boulevardier's trio of ingredients but changes up the original ratio. "Instead of the usual equal parts, I have upped the whiskey and dialed down the other two," he says. "This really lets the bourbon shine. I also like to use Carpano Antica instead of a standard red vermouth. The Carpano adds a bit of weight and an extra layer of bitterness, creating a very well-balanced cocktail."

For two bold takes on this classic cocktail, see the recipes for the Wagyu & Chocolate Boulevardier on page 242 and the Crème Brûlée Boulevardier on page 89.

◆

GLASSWARE: Old-fashioned glass
GARNISH: Orange peel

- 1½ oz. (45 ml) Heaven's Door Bourbon
- ¾ oz. (22.5 ml) Carpano Antica Formula Vermouth
- ¾ oz. (22.5 ml) Campari

1. Add all of the ingredients to a mixing pitcher.

2. Add ice and gently stir.

3. Strain the cocktail into an old-fashioned glass over a big ice cube, express the oils from an orange peel, and drop the peel inside the glass to garnish.

A TOUCH OF TIKI

Recreating the past is a tricky gambit to get right. How do you concoct an authentic, if not nostalgic, experience for an era when most of today's cocktail enthusiasts weren't even alive? (Of course, that same sentiment holds true for all the classics already called out in this chapter.) Vancouver flirted with tiki culture in the 1960s, when Trader Vic's iconic Polynesian-style restaurant opened on the shores of Coal Harbour downtown. It was an import—like tiki bars themselves—from our neighbors to the south. (Ceramic mugs typical in tiki bars in the United States are held in the collections of the Smithsonian's National Museum of American History.)

The iconic triangular-shaped building was situated in a parking lot near where The Westin Bayshore hotel sits today. In the 1990s, the restaurant was shuttered and the building was full-scale floated out into Coal Harbour en route to Vancouver Island, like a wayward traveler who knew it was time to move on.

COBRA'S FANG

Tiki culture has enjoyed a second coming in the city. For ten years, the Shameful Tiki Room has been channeling that sense of escape Vancouver embraced decades ago. A place where we can peer through vintage-tinted glasses at a paradise overflowing with creative cocktails that are in a class of their own. Each cocktail is made as true to the original recipe as possible with fresh citrus, and house-made syrups (sold under the Shameful Syrup Co. label) and drams.

It's all part of the experience of sharing a smoky Volcano Bowl, sipping a Zombie, Painkiller, or the sinister-sounding Cobra's Fang. Rod Moore, owner of the Shameful Tiki Room, describes this classic tiki created by "Don the Beachcomber" around 1937 as "one of Donn Beach's very early recipes; it showcases his incredible creativity with multiple complex ingredients like falernum and fassionola. The Shameful Tiki Room specializes in bringing recipes like this back to life as accurately as possible, giving our guests the chance to experience cocktails not easily made or found."

GLASSWARE: Collins glass
GARNISH: Lime wheel, mint sprig

- 2½ oz. (75 ml) fassionola syrup
- 1½ oz. (45 ml) dark rum
- 1½ oz. (45 ml) fresh lime juice
- ½ oz. (15 ml) 151-proof demerara rum
- ½ oz. (15 ml) Shameful Syrup Co. Falernum
- ½ oz. (15 ml) orange juice
- 1 dash Angostura bitters
- 6 drops Pernod

1. In a mixing tin, combine all of the ingredients. Add a cup of crushed ice, then flash-blend for five seconds. An immersion stick blender works well. If you use a countertop blender, pulse carefully—don't overmix!

2. Pour everything into the collins glass; add crushed ice to fill.

3. Garnish with the lime wheel and mint sprig.

CLASSICS REDUX

ESPRESSO MANHATTAN

BEE ON YOUR KNEES

PORTUGUESE OLD FASHIONED

PAPER PLANE

PENICILLIN

LAVENDER GIN FIZZ

CRÈME BRÛLÉE BOULEVARDIER

EL CHAPULÍN

LA BELLA

ROYAL SPRITZ

PIMM'S CUP

VESPER

JALISCO MARTINI

GOVERNOR SOUR

WINTER DAIQUIRI

There's always a temptation to hack the classics, whether it involves making incremental improvements or doing complete teardowns. In the right hands, many are rebuilt better. Yet, the age of influence often threatens to take it too far, luring curious imbibers into the dark web of drinking. For instance, it's easy to agree with one writer's sentiment on the best way to make a Dirty Shirley: Don't. And why are there so many hot takes on the ultimate Italian summer staple—the Spritz—including one questionable magazine directive to actually "make it hot!"? Is swapping out chilled and effervescent Prosecco for white wine and warming up the Aperol-based cocktail an alternative—or an oxymoron?

The cocktails in this chapter have some roots in the originals—both classic and modern—with both bold and subtle tweaks from the pros. Like introducing elderflower liqueur to a Bee's Knees or substituting some of the old-world Scotch in a Penicillin for new-world Vancouver-made whiskey. Bartenders ultimately know what elements play well together, especially with cocktails making a comeback. Alannah Taylor puts a sophisticated Italian twist on the Cosmopolitan. And Adam Domet marries Dick Bradsell's 1983-born Espresso Martini with the classic Manhattan. The result of this cocktail comingling is an Espresso Manhattan, a high-velocity lovechild that might even outshine its parents.

ESPRESSO MANHATTAN

POURHOUSE, GASTOWN

Brick by brick, Vancouver's historic buildings are fading into obscurity as the city continues its nonstop evolution into a forest of glass and steel. But at Pourhouse in Vancouver's first neighborhood, Gastown (named for a saloon owner, see page 13), the past is preserved with reverence.

Situated in a 1910 building (an old-timer for Vancouver) that was once home to Leckie Boot Company (it outfitted the era's miners, loggers, and fishermen with footwear and supplied boots to the Canadian Armed Forces), Pourhouse is dominated by the thirty-eight-foot bar handcrafted from reclaimed century-old Douglas fir planks. Antiques from yesteryear bring a time-honored quality to the room, but don't mistake the bar as merely a throwback.

Pourhouse bar manager Adam Domet says his Espresso Manhattan is an elegant update "inspired by the re-emergence of the timeless Espresso Martini with a richer depth of flavour and complexity of Angel's Envy Port Finished Bourbon." For coffee-crazed Vancouverites, it's a welcome return to a trend that this time around is sure to stay.

GLASSWARE: Coupe glass, chilled

GARNISH: Cacao powder

- 1½ oz. (45 ml) Angel's Envy Kentucky Straight Bourbon Whiskey Finished in Port Barrels
- 1½ oz. (45 ml) chilled espresso
- ¾ oz. (22.5 ml) Coffee & Cherries (see recipe below)
- ½ oz. (15 ml) Simple Syrup (see recipe below)
- 2 dashes Scrappy's Chocolate Bitters

1. In a cocktail shaker, combine all of the ingredients. Shake hard for 8 seconds until well chilled.

2. Fine-strain the cocktail into the chilled coupe using a Hawthorne or julep strainer and a small sieve.

3. Garnish with a light dusting of cacao powder.

COFFEE AND CHERRIES: In a clean container, combine 2 oz. (60 ml) coffee liqueur, 2 oz. (60 ml) late-bottle vintage ruby port, and 2 oz. (60 ml) cherry brandy.

SIMPLE SYRUP: In a pot, combine ½ cup (100 grams) turbinado sugar and ½ cup (100 grams) cold water. On medium heat, stir until the sugar is dissolved, bringing it to a boil. Allow it to cool, then bottle it and refrigerate.

SPY VS. SOCIALITE

> "In vino veritas, so often quoted, does not mean that
> a man will tell the truth when in drink but will reveal
> the hidden side of his character."
> —Frank Meier

The question of who invented the Bee's Knees is another cocktail co-nundrum, with origins attributed to two larger-than-life characters. One is Frank Meier, head bartender at the eponymous bar inside Par-is's opulent Hôtel Ritz. The other, an American socialite and philan-thropist named Margaret Brown, aka "The Unsinkable Molly Brown." For those not in the know, Brown's "unsinkable" moniker refers to her surviving the 1912 iceberg strike that sent the RMS *Titanic* to the bottom of the North Atlantic, about 400 miles from Newfoundland and Labrador where the ship still rests today.

But back to the bartender. The Austrian-born chap was known as much for his conviviality as his cocktail cred. He started working in the bar in 1921 (until 1947) and wrote *The Artistry of Mixing Drinks*, which was published in 1936. If you flip to page 25, there's the Bee's Knees cocktail, bearing the signature M icon that denotes recipes Meier him-self created. He writes, "In shaker: the juice of one-quarter lemon, a teaspoon of honey, one-half glass of gin; shake well and serve."

But cocktail historian Jared Brown has recently revealed newfound evidence that Molly Brown (hailed as a hero for helping rescue passen-gers aboard the luxury ship) is the true creator of the Bee's Knees. He points to an April 22, 1929, article published in the *Standard Union*, discussing socialites who frequented so-called "women's bars" that were said to be "opening on every corner in downtown Paris." It stated: "The 'Bees' Knees' is an invention of Mrs. J. J. Brown . . . and is a rather sweet combination including honey and lemon."

Brown died in 1932, four years before Meier's book was published. Could he have ripped off her recipe? Who knows? However, that might be the least interesting thing about Meier. He was allegedly a spy who helped both the French resistance and British spies, according to *The Hotel on Place Vendome: Life, Death, and Betrayal at the Hotel Ritz in Paris*. Written by Dr. Tilar J. Mazzeo, an author, historian, and winemaker who lives on Vancouver Island, the best-selling book says the Jewish bartender also passed coded messages for the German resistance, and that the failed plot to assassinate Adolf Hitler was likely hatched over cocktails made by Meier.

BEE ON YOUR KNEES

KEY PARTY, MOUNT PLEASANT

The naughtily named Bee on Your Knees cocktail, crafted at Key Party, a speakeasy (see page 284) hidden on Main Street in Mount Pleasant, isn't exactly faithful to America's Prohibition-era classic, whether Meier or Mrs. Brown's. This one is still shaken up and silky, but it goes beyond the quotidian London dry gin, swapping it for international award-winning Ungava. This Canadian gin is distilled in northern Quebec and uses six types of foraged Arctic botanicals, including Nordic juniper, wild rose hip, and cloudberry, from which it gets its bold yellow hue. Find a zero-proof version of the classic on page 346.

GLASSWARE: Coupe glass, chilled

GARNISH: Angostura bitters

- 2 oz. (60 ml) Ungava Gin
- 1 oz. (30 ml) St-Germain Elderflower Liqueur
- 1 oz. (30 ml) egg white
- 1 oz. (30 ml) lemon juice
- 1 oz. (30 ml) Honey Syrup (see recipe opposite)

1. Add all of the ingredients to a shaker without ice. Dry-shake.

2. Add ice and shake.

3. Double-strain the cocktail into the chilled coupe.

4. In a sweeping motion, add a few lines of bitters, using a straw or pick to draw pretty designs.

HONEY SYRUP: In a small pot, add 2⅕ pounds (1 kilogram) honey to 3 cups (700 ml) water. Let sit on medium heat until the honey is mixed.

PORTUGUESE OLD FASHIONED

THE LIBERTY DISTILLERY, GRANVILLE ISLAND

If you change up even one ingredient in a classic, does it become an altogether new cocktail? It's easy to argue each side, but this Portuguese-tinged take from The Liberty Distillery (see the Distillers + Makers chapter beginning on page 107) on Granville Island is clearly a contender in both camps. It mostly sticks to the original formula and method but employs its own Trust Single Cask Madeira Whiskey (a limited release) and opts for grapefruit bitters instead of the traditional Angostura. Like all of The Liberty Distillery's spirits, this whiskey uses organic, 100 percent BC-grown grain and is tripled-distilled, then aged for three years entirely in ex-Madeira casks.

GLASSWARE: Rocks glass
GARNISH: Swath of orange peel, 2 maraschino cherries on a pick

- 2 oz. (60 ml) Trust Whiskey– Single Cask Madeira
- 2 sugar cubes
- 4 to 5 dashes Scrappy's Grapefruit Bitters

1. Chill a rocks glass.

2. Place a napkin over a mixing glass. Place the sugar cubes on the napkin, douse the sugar cubes with the grapefruit bitters, and tip the sugar cubes into your mixing glass.

3. Using a muddler, smash and swirl the sugar cubes until you've formed a paste of sorts. Add the whiskey and continue to swirl the ingredients until your muddler comes up clean.

4. Fill a mixing glass with ice and stir until well chilled and until the sugar is mostly dissolved. Strain the cocktail into the chilled rocks glass over fresh ice and garnish with the orange peel and cherries.

ADDICTIVE AMARI

Both Amaro Nonino Quintessentia and Amaro Montenegro noted in the Paper Plane cocktail versions are considered mild and mild-to-medium when it comes to their level of bitterness. They're gateway choices when exploring the addictive family of bitter (*amaro* in Italian) herbal spirits collectively called *amari*. The sheer volume of these bitter elixirs available (mostly from Italy) offers endless experimenting along a spectrum that ranges from pleasingly bitter to the extreme.

Like Malört, a Swedish wormwood liquor described as "citrus-flavored gasoline," or the most medicinal-tasting spirit I've had, Unicum, made with more than forty herbs and spices and which has been around for 200 years. Apologies to the Zwack family and my own Hungarian relations, but this drink is a pine-resin punch in the face. However, its backstory is a trip worth taking.

What makes bitters, well, bitter? The answer is a range of what are called bittering agents, the common ones being gentian (an alpine plant), cinchona bark (quinine is extracted from it), rhubarb, artichoke (Cynar is a popular brand of amari), and wormwood (a key ingredient in absinthe). Here's the thing, though: drinking amari straight—whether on the rocks or neat—is a delicious way to sip it as an aperitif or digestif and detect the nuances of each. But crawl before you run. Do incorporate extreme bitters into your repertoire, but start with small quantities, tasting and tinkering like the pros do.

PAPER PLANE

Back in 2008, Australian bartender Sam Ross created the original Paper Plane at The Violet Hour in Chicago using equal parts of four key ingredients: bourbon, Campari, grappa-based Amaro Nonino Quintessentia, and lemon juice. By all accounts, though, Ross thought the Campari was a little too aggressive, so he replaced it with the sweeter, lower-alcohol, and less bitter Aperol.

The version below, crafted at Hawksworth Bar, which is ensconced inside the swanky 1927 Rosewood Hotel Georgia, adheres to Ross's rework with one subtle shift. Instead of Nonino, it employs Amaro Montenegro, which is less complex but still approachable with bitter, sweet, orange, and herbaceous qualities.

GLASS: Coupe glass, chilled

- ¾ oz. (22.5 ml) Bulleit Bourbon
- ¾ oz. (22.5 ml) Aperol
- ¾ oz. (22.5 ml) Amaro Montenegro
- ¾ oz. (22.5 ml) lemon juice

1. Shake all of the ingredients together with ice.

2. Strain the cocktail into the chilled coupe.

PENICILLIN

BAYSIDE LOUNGE, WEST END

A nother American invention. Another riff with a local touch. In fact, Sam Ross's Penicillin was a riff on a Gold Rush, which was itself a riff on a Whiskey Sour (see page 266). It's like a matryoshka doll of drinks where one is born from another and another . . . Dez Haffenden's version from the Bayside Lounge plays with the original proportions a little, upping the three-quarter ounce of each lemon juice and honey syrup to one ounce. And although Ross's used two types of Scotch, Haffenden reaches for Odd Society's single-malt whiskey, made from 100 percent BC-grown malted barley.

GLASSWARE: Old-fashioned glass
GARNISH: Burnt lemon peel

- 2 oz. (60 ml) Odd Society Commodore Canadian Single Malt Whisky
- 1 oz. (30 ml) Honey Syrup (see recipe below)
- 1 oz. (30 ml) lemon juice
- ½ oz. (15 ml) Laphroaig Single Malt Whisky
- ½ teaspoon (2.5 ml) ground ginger

1. Thoroughly shake all of the ingredients with ice, except the Laphroaig.

2. Double-strain the cocktail into the old-fashioned glass filled with ice.

3. Float the Laphroaig on top.

HONEY SYRUP: Mix together 2 parts honey to 1 part hot water. Store it in the refrigerator for up to a week.

THE FIZZ FAMILY

Countless sources point to the "father of American mixology," bartender Jerry Thomas, as having created the classic Gin Fizz, the recipe for which was first published in the 1887 edition of his book *The Bar-Tender's Guide*. And they're right. Mostly. This cocktail first came to light in his book as the "fiz," made with various spirits. But the original Gin Fizz (with the double "z") as we've come to know it—crowned with frothy egg whites and elevated by soda water—was actually called the Silver Fiz in Thomas's tome. His original Gin Fizz recipe didn't include egg whites or soda, and it specified Holland Gin, while the Silver Fiz called for Old Tom Gin.

LAVENDER GIN FIZZ

THE NARROW LOUNGE, EAST VANCOUVER

The Narrow Lounge in East Vancouver is so unassuming it's hard to locate if you're not in the know (find out in chapter 9—Speakeasies & Hidden Bars). But the secret has long been out; the bar opened way back in 2007 and has been luring locals ever since. In 2022, this skinny parlor with a pint-sized patio climbed the ranks of Canada's 100 Best Bars, shaking and stirring its way to 44th place. The Lavender Gin Fizz brings an extra hint of botanicals to this class cocktail, which is not traditionally served over ice, making it especially quaffable on Vancouver's hot summer days (it happens).

GLASSWARE: Double rocks glass, chilled

GARNISH: Lavender buds, dehydrated lemon wedge

- 2 oz. (60 ml) Lavender Gin (see recipe below)
- 1 oz. (30 ml) egg white
- 1 oz. (30 ml) lemon Juice
- ¾ oz. (22.5 ml) Simple Syrup (see recipe below)
- Soda water, to top

1. Shake all of the ingredients together without ice.

2. Add ice and shake again.

3. Double-strain the cocktail into the chilled double rocks glass.

4. Top with soda water.

LAVENDER GIN: Add ½ cup (125 ml) of lavender buds to a bottle of your favorite gin. Let it sit for 6 hours. Strain.

SIMPLE SYRUP: In a pot, mix 1 cup (250 ml) of sugar with 1 cup (250 ml) of water. Stir over medium heat until the sugar is dissolved. Allow the syrup to cool then store it in the refrigerator.

CRÈME BRÛLÉE BOULEVARDIER

GASTRONOMY GASTOWN, GASTOWN

Gastronomy Gastown only opened its doors in early 2023, but is settling into its spot on East Cordova Street, promising a laid-back atmosphere: "Italy meets modern-day Vancouver." Offerings include the In the Eye of the Gods, a bitter and spicy Negroni riff, and the decadent Crème Brûlée Boulevardier.

GLASSWARE: Nick & Nora glass
GARNISH: Banana, crème-brûléed

- 1½ oz. (45 ml) Crown Royal Northern Harvest Rye
- ⅔ oz. (20 ml) Giffard Banane du Brésil liqueur
- ⅓ oz. (10 ml) Campari
- ⅓ oz. (10 ml) Amontillado sherry
- ⅓ oz. (10 ml) Antica Formula Vermouth
- 1 dash Ms. Better's Bitters Banana Bergamot
- 1 dash chocolate bitters

1. To crème-brûlée the banana, cut a thin slice, sprinkle some raw sugar on it, then torch to add a brûléed effect.

2. Pour all of the ingredients into a stirring glass. Add ice and stir for approximately 30 seconds or until it the mixture is properly diluted.

3. Strain the cocktail into the Nick & Nora glass and garnish with the brûléed banana.

EL CHAPULÍN

GRAPES & SODA, SOUTH GRANVILLE

Smoky, spicy, and chocolaty are the words Satoshi Yonemori uses to describe his take on a Grasshopper. The award-winning bartender and co-owner of Grapes & Soda (and Farmer's Apprentice restaurant next door) has flipped this old oddball desert drink on its head by introducing tequila—thus its Spanish name—instead of vodka. Yonemori skips the cloying crème de mint from the original but uses white crème de cacao, spruce syrup, and a tiny bit of Thai chiles, offsetting that hit of spice with some pineapple and lime.

GLASSWARE: Large-stem glass

GARNISH: Lime wheel, lime zest, Thai chile

- 2 oz. (60 ml) Profesor mezcal
- 1 oz. (30 ml) lime juice
- ⅔ oz. (20 ml) Spruce Syrup (see recipe below)
- ½ oz. (15 ml) egg white
- ¼ oz. (7.5 ml) white crème de cacao
- 4 pieces of fresh pineapple
- 1 thin slice of Thai chile
- 3 dashes Angostura bitters

1. Use a hand blender to mix all of the ingredients in a shaker. This will whip the egg white and blitz the Thai chile.

2. Add ice. Shake well and double-strain the cocktail into a large-stem glass.

3. Garnish with the lime wheel, lime zest, and extra Thai chile.

SPRUCE SYRUP: Blend together 1½ tablespoons (20 grams) of picked and washed Canadian spruce tips, 4¼ cups (1,000 grams) organic cane sugar, 3⅓ cups (800 ml) filtered water, and $^{17}/_{20}$ cup (200 grams) ice until the sugar dissolves. Fine-strain. Let sit for a few minutes. Skim the foam from the mixture. Vacuum-pack and freeze the syrup. Thaw when needed.

LA BELLA

CAPO & THE SPRITZ, YALETOWN

Alannah Taylor, bar manager at Capo & the Spritz (inside the Opus Hotel), fondly recalls a memory of watching her mother sipping on Cosmopolitans, noting she had always wanted to try the "pink and pretty" drink. Although the Cosmo was born in the late 1980s, the cocktail only really came into its own during the zeitgeist of *Sex and the City* a decade later. And while reboots often leave something to be desired, Taylor's hits the mark.

GLASSWARE: Nick & Nora glass
GARNISH: Edible rose petals

- 1½ oz. (45 ml) Absolut Vodka
- 1½ oz. (45 ml) Ms. Better's Bitters Miraculous Foamer
- 1 oz. (30 ml) freshly pressed lime juice
- 1 oz. (30 ml) Cranberry Syrup (see recipe opposite)
- ½ oz. (15 ml) Hotel Starlino Rosé Aperitivo
- 1 dash Dillon's Orange Bitters

1. Combine all of the ingredients in a shaker without ice. Dry-shake vigorously, add ice, and shake again.

2. Fine-strain the cocktail into a Nick & Nora glass.

3. Spritz an orange peel over the cocktail then discard the peel. Line edible rose petals down the middle for the garnish.

CRANBERRY SYRUP: In a pot, combine 1 cup (250 ml) cranberries, 4¼ cups (1,000 ml) granulated white sugar, and 4¼ cups (1,000 ml) water. Bring the mixture to a boil, then reduce heat and simmer for 10 minutes until the cranberries start to burst. Remove from heat, and strain through a fine mesh sieve, pushing the cranberries through as much as you can.

ROYAL SPRITZ

CAPO & THE SPRITZ, YALETOWN

The Royal Spritz is a refreshing eye-catcher, says Alannah Taylor. "Empress 1908, as one of the most popular beautiful 'blue' local gins of British Columbia, is expertly highlighted in this twist on a classic Gin & Tonic. St-Germaine offers an elderflower hint, and the tartness of the lemon plays with the bitterness of the tonic poured over locally crafted polarized ice cubes."

GLASSWARE: Rocks glass

GARNISH: Dehydrated lemon, edible rosebud

- 1½ oz. (45 ml) Empress 1908 Gin
- 1 oz. (30 ml) fresh squeezed lemon juice
- ½ oz. (15 ml) St-Germain Elderflower Liqueur
- 1 barspoon (2.5 ml) simple syrup
- Kodama Ice Co polarized ice cube
- Fever-Tree Tonic, to top

1. Combine all of the ingredients, except the tonic, in a shaker with ice.

2. Vigorously shake, and fine-strain the cocktail into the rocks glass over the ice cube.

3. Top with the tonic, and garnish with the dehydrated lemon with a rosebud placed in the middle.

PIMM'S CUP

BELGARD KITCHEN, RAILTOWN

Alexa Greenman is clear about how she feels about the classic that's long been served at the Wimbledon tennis tournament but has hardly become a hit in North America. "It's my belief that the Pimm's is an entirely underrated cocktail," she says. The bar director continues: "Our small change is to lean more into those spiced and citrus notes with the addition of lemon juice and falernum, a rich spiced syrup often used in tiki cocktails. We pay homage to the original by making sure to accentuate the garnish with the addition of aromatic rosemary and lemon as well as the drink's iconic cucumber presence. The result is a multifaceted ode to a drink that still manages to be refreshing after all these years."

GLASSWARE: Round-bottomed collins glass
GARNISH: Lemon slice, rosemary sprig

- Cucumber slice
- 2 oz. (60 ml) Pimm's No. 1 Cup
- ½ oz. (15 ml) Giffard Falernum
- ½ oz. (15 ml) lemon juice
- 4 oz. (120 ml) Boylan's Ginger Soda, to top

1. Add the cucumber slice to the collins glass. Top with ice.

2. Add the Pimm's, falernum, and lemon juice. Top with the ginger soda.

3. Garnish with the lemon slice and rosemary sprig.

STIRRED, NOT SHAKEN

Not all rules are meant to be broken and knowing when to stir or shake is super simple, though not without its dissenters. When a cocktail's ingredients are mostly spirits (meaning no citrus, egg whites, or creamy liqueurs), stir them over ice long enough to mix the elements and chill and dilute the drink while maintaining its silky texture. It's the preferred method, of course, for the Martini, as well as the Manhattan, Negroni, and Old-Fashioned.

VESPER

BELGARD KITCHEN, RAILTOWN

Another updated classic has made it onto the menu at Belgard Kitchen. This time, it's James Bond's iconic order, the Vesper, reinvented in a less boozy way, which Q would surely approve of. The Belgard team says the drink already has a strong foundation with the gin, so their secret weapon involves retiring the vodka and deputizing Martini Bianco. The bright, citrusy, and aromatic vermouth complements similar flavors from the Lillet but with a greener finish, giving the Vesper a slightly more approachable finish.

GLASSWARE: Coupe glass
GARNISH: Lemon twist

- 2 oz. (60 ml) Beefeater Gin
- ½ oz. (15 ml) Lillet Blanc
- ½ oz. (15 ml) Martini Bianco
- Lemon oil

1. Chill the coupe glass and set it aside.

2. Place all of the ingredients into a stirring vessel. Add ice. Stir for 10 to 15 seconds.

3. Strain into the chilled coupe.

4. Spritz with lemon oil and garnish with the lemon twist.

JALISCO MARTINI

HAVANA, COMMERCIAL DRIVE

Situated on the always buzzing strip of Commercial Drive in Vancouver's "Little Italy," Havana Restaurant is awash in tequila, with Margaritas and Verdita shots making up the majority of its cocktail orders.

Bar director Alexa Greenman says the flavor combinations in this cocktail might at first seem unorthodox, but the pairings such as tequila and orange, orange and chocolate, and chocolate and coffee play well, thus the Jalisco Martini was born. "Savory, sweet, bright, and balanced, this drink gives you the edge you need to start your night . . . or perhaps keep it going."

GLASSWARE: Coupe glass, chilled
GARNISH: Cocoa nibs

- 1 oz. (30 ml) Coffee, Cacao, and Vanilla-Infused Altos Tequila (see recipe at right)
- ½ oz. (15 ml) Chocolate Liqueur (see recipe below)
- ½ oz. (15 ml) Kahlua
- ½ oz. (15 ml) orange Juice
- Double shot of Milano Espresso

1. Add all of the ingredients to a shaker tin and shake vigorously.

2. Double-strain the cocktail into the chilled coupe glass.

3. Garnish one-third of the cocktail with a sprinkle of cacao nibs.

CHOCOLATE LIQUEUR: Combine 1 cup (250 ml) of cacao nibs with 2 cups (500 ml) of Wray and Nephew White Overproof Rum. Seal and shake. Allow the infusion to set for 3 days minimum. Strain out the solids. Next, add ½ cup (125 ml) of water, ½ cup (125 ml) of Crème de Cacao, and ½ cup (125 ml) of Vanilla Syrup (see recipe below) to the liqueur.

VANILLA SYRUP: Combine 1 oz. (30 ml) vanilla extract with ½ cup (125 ml) of a 1:1 simple syrup.

COFFEE-INFUSED TEQUILA: Slice one vanilla bean vertically and add one half to a 25 ½ oz. (750 ml) bottle of Altos Tequila. Let the mixture infuse for at least 24 hours. Remove vanilla bean. Pour vanilla-infused tequila (keep the bottle) into separate sealable container. Add 3.5 oz (105 ml) ground Milano "Bourbon" coffee. Let sit for 48 hours. Strain coffee-tequila mixture through a filter. Add 3.5 oz. (104 ml) of Demerara Syrup to the liquid and funnel back into Altos Tequila bottle.

DEMERARA SYRUP: Mix 3 ½ oz. (100 ml) of demerara sugar with 8 oz. (240 ml) of hot water.

GOVERNOR SOUR

HAVANA, COMMERCIAL DRIVE

The classic Pisco Sour gets a tropical twist with the addition of coconut and passion fruit syrup, while maintaining a uniquely sweetened and lightly tart flavour profile, says Havana bar director Alexa Greenman. Its namesake is El Gobernador Pisco, which translates in English to "The Governor." The bar team adds a playful touch with edible artwork that transports guests to warmer climates. "This drink tends to be an #IFKYK moment in that its edible image is unique to Havana alone. With careful sourcing of edible paper, ink, and the perfect tropical image, this drink stands out on any table or any Instagram story."

GLASSWARE: Coupe glass, chilled
GARNISH: Edible artwork

- 2 oz. (60 ml) El Gobernador Pisco
- 1 oz. (30 ml) lime juice
- ½ oz (15 ml) Passion Fruit Syrup (see recipe at right)
- ½ oz (15 ml) Giffard Coconut Syrup
- 1 oz. egg white (about one egg)

1. Add all of the ingredients to a shaker tin and dry-shake.

2. Add ice and wet-shake.

3. Double-strain the cocktail into a chilled coupe.

4. Garnish with an edible image. Lightly spritz with water to set the art.

PASSION FRUIT SYRUP: Make 6 cups (1.5 liters) of a 1:1 simple syrup. Add ½ pound (225 grams) of passion fruit puree to the simple syrup. Bring the mixture to a boil, then let it simmer for 15 minutes. Remove it from heat and allow it to cool before using it.

WINTER DAIQUIRI

NOTCH8 RESTAURANT & BAR, FAIRMONT HOTEL VANCOUVER, DOWNTOWN

When the Fairmont Hotel Vancouver opened in 1939, the classic daiquiri had already been invented hundred of miles away, in the 1800s. Like the hotel itself, which has been given modern tweaks—with Notch8 Restaurant and Bar as part of its latest contemporary redesign—so has this summer staple cocktail. It gets an elegant seasonal makeover that's sure to brighten gray days with warm spices and tart cranberries.

GLASSWARE: Coupe glass

GARNISH: Candied (or regular) cranberries

- **2 oz. (60 ml) Bacardi White Rum**
- **1 oz. (30 ml) cranberry juice**
- **¾ oz. (22.5 ml) Winter Syrup (see recipe at right)**
- **½ oz. (15 ml) lime juice**

1. Combine all of the ingredients in a shaker and shake with ice.

2. Strain the cocktail into a coupe glass.

3. Garnish with cranberries.

WINTER SYRUP: In a small saucepan on medium-high heat, combine 1 cup (250 ml) simple syrup, 4 cloves, 4 allspice berries, 4 star anise, 3 cinnamon sticks (broken), and 2 vanilla bean pods (split and seeded). Bring the mixture to a simmer for 15 to 20 minutes. Remove the pan from heat, strain the syrup through a sieve, and allow it to cool before using.

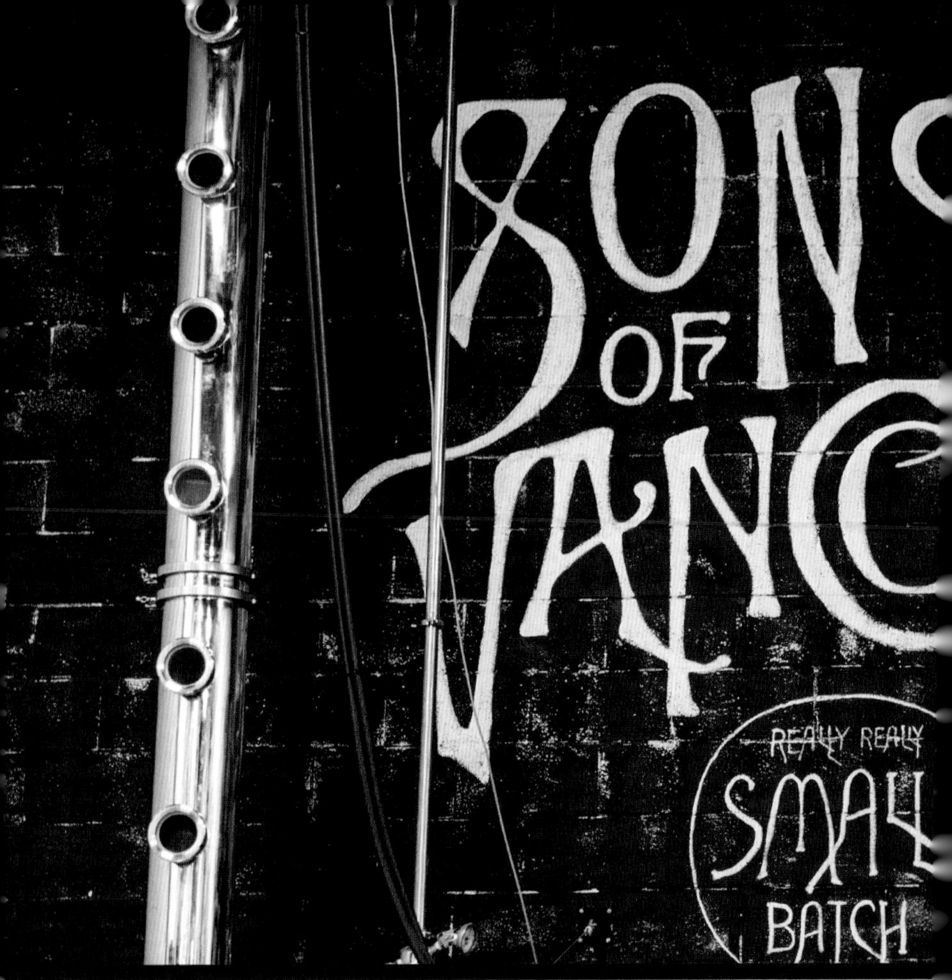
OF
REALLY REALLY
SMALL
BATCH

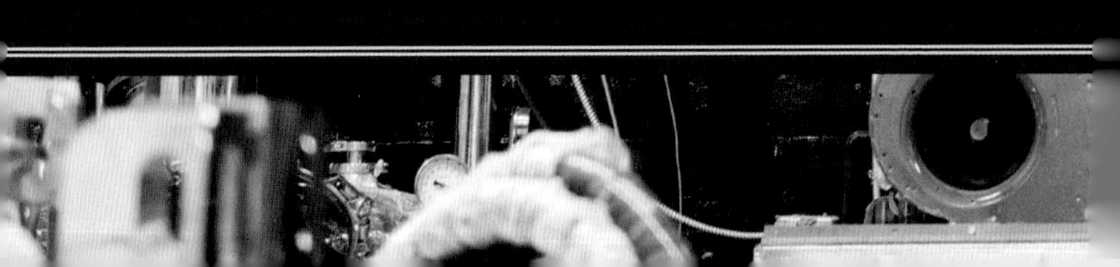

DISTILLERS + MAKERS

SOV AMARETTO SOUR

NORTH SHORE MULE

CORPSE REVIVER NO. BLUE

WINTER VACAY

BLACK MANHATTAN

LIBERTY'S NEW YORK SOUR

LIBERTY'S BURGUNDY SUNSET

VIOLET & CLAIRE

ELDER FASHION

ESPRESSO MARTINI CANADIANA

KARDEMUMMA

COPPERPENNY GIN & STORMY

GIN & TONIC

PEGU CLUB IN THE WOODS

Alex Hamer was tired of working in technology and decided to open a distillery. But instead of making spirits, he found himself championing the craft distilling industry in BC and beyond. In 2014, Hamer founded BC Distilled, an annual event that brings together artisan distilleries. It gives the public a chance to meet the makers and sample their products all in one place. Hamer didn't have a grand vision for the inaugural BC Distilled—he simply created an event he would want to go to.

"I was convinced the industry was going to grow. I didn't know where, but I knew it would grow," says Hamer. "And distillers were really treated like second-class citizens. We always had one or two distilleries at a wine festival or at a beer festival. I thought, wouldn't it be cool to have one that's just distilleries."

Before the BC government updated its craft distilling policy in 2013, there were only about twenty distilleries in the province. The previous tax structure meant they were all treated as commercial distilleries. Hamer shares an anecdote to illustrate: one gin distiller said that for every bottle of booze he sold, he lost $1. The new policy defined the differences between commercial and craft, setting out specific criteria and benefits for both.

To qualify as "craft," distilleries must use 100 percent BC agricultural inputs in the production of all their products. There are limits to how much alcohol they can produce annually, among other rules. In 2015, distilleries with lounges were allowed to sell up to 20 percent of their liquor not produced on-site, which helped distilleries expand their cocktail offerings.

There are still huge hurdles for craft distillers, but the community is mutually supportive, says Hamer. "They are talking to each other, they're experimenting, they're sharing ideas, they're trying each other's products." That drive and innovation can only push the industry forward. "I think there's an argument to be made that British Columbia is leading the way in distilling in Canada."

The distillers and makers highlighted in this chapter have shared their stories and recipes, showcasing their passion for producing spirits, liqueurs, bitters, and even artisanal ice. Many of them have garnered awards and recognition in BC and well beyond, a testament to the high-caliber quality that can be found right in Vancouver's backyard. Additional recipes from distilleries as well as other bars and restaurants working with their products are scattered throughout the chapters with intel on ingredients such as grains, botanicals, and more.

SONS OF VANCOUVER DISTILLERY

Cigarettes on a Leather Jacket (2021). Marshmallows Over a Campfire (2022). Palm Trees and a Tropical Breeze (2023). The names on the first three whiskey releases from Sons of Vancouver Distillery instantly evoke emotions. They sound provocative and playful, but these small-batch spirits have won some serious awards.

At the 2023 Canadian Whisky Awards, Palm Trees and a Tropical Breeze was named Canadian Whisky of the Year. It's an understatement to say the accolade is unusual for a distiller of its size. Judging for the competition involves a blind tasting by a panel of nine whiskey experts, and this is the first time in the thirteen-year history of the competition an artisan producer—not to mention one of the smallest in Canada—has netted the number one spot. The 100 percent rye aged in ex-bourbon barrels and finished in Caribbean rum casks won three other awards at the 2023 event.

You'll have to wait for the next release to get your hands on a bottle of SOV's whiskey. But some of the spirits introduced when the independent distillery opened in 2015 are included in the recipes below and in the cocktails served at its tasting room in North Vancouver. And if you want to learn more about making spirits, sign up for workshop at the Sons of Vancouver Distillery School, where you'll spend five days working alongside SOV's team, getting hands-on with everything from mashing and distilling to bottling and labeling.

SOV AMARETTO SOUR

SONS OF VANCOUVER DISTILLERY, NORTH VANCOUVER

The Amaretto Sour is often overlooked as a classic cocktail, but when made correctly it is not too sweet, not too sour, and deliciously velvety. Sons of Vancouver has had an amaretto sour on its tasting room menu since they opened, and it remains their most requested cocktail by far. This version, from founder James Lester, uses house amaretto and swaps out the lemon for lime. The addition of Angostura bitters rounds out the flavor profile and works as a perfect garnish.

GLASSWARE: Coupe glass, chilled

GARNISH: Bitters (optional)

- 1½ oz. (45 ml) Sons of Vancouver No. 82 Amaretto Liqueur
- ¾ oz. (20 ml) fresh lime juice
- 1 egg white, about 1 oz. (30 ml)
- 3 dashes Angostura bitters

1. Add all of the ingredients to a shaker tin and dry-shake (no ice) for 30 seconds.

2. Add ice to the tin and shake again until the tin feels cold and has condensation on the outside.

3. Double-strain the cocktail into the chilled coupe.

4. Add a few drops of bitters on top and swirl with a toothpick in a circle (optional).

NORTH SHORE MULE

SONS OF VANCOUVER DISTILLERY, NORTH VANCOUVER

E asily its most divisive product, Sons of Vancouver says its Chili Vodka is a love-it-or-hate-it kind of spirit. Made with bird's eye chiles (the kind used commonly in Thai cooking), it's spicy to say the least. When added to a Mule, the heat of the chiles enhances the prickly warmth of the ginger at the back of your throat.

GLASSWARE: Copper mug

GARNISH: Mint sprig, 2 lime wheels

- 1½ oz. (45 ml) Sons of Vancouver Vodka Vodka Vodka
- ½ oz. (15 ml) Sons of Vancouver Chili Vodka
- ½ oz. (15 ml) fresh lime juice
- 2 dashes Angostura bitters
- Ginger beer (Reed's or similar), to top

1. Add the spirits and lime juice to the mug; fill with ice.

2. Top with the ginger beer and stir.

3. Garnish with a mint spring and two fresh or dehydrated lime wheels.

CORPSE REVIVER NO. BLUE

SONS OF VANCOUVER DISTILLERY, NORTH VANCOUVER

Sons of Vancouver's annual spirits release for April Fool's Day is its most anticipated of traditions. Each year, the distillery takes a commonly known bottom-shelf liqueur and flips it on its head to provide a hyper-craft, tongue-in-cheek version of the original. One of their first and most popular offerings is the craft blue curaçao. The Corpse Reviver No. Blue, a cheeky take on an old classic, was first poured in 2007 in New York City by Jacob Briars. It's been adapted here to feature Sons of Vancouver spirits.

GLASSWARE: Martini or coupe glass, chilled
GARNISH: Lemon twist (optional)

- ¾ oz. (22.5 ml) Sons of Vancouver Junicopia Gin
- ¾ oz. (22.5 ml) Sons of Vancouver Blue Curaçao
- ¾ oz. (22.5 ml) Lillet Blanc
- ¾ oz. (22.5 ml) fresh lemon juice
- 1 barspoon of absinthe or Pernod

1. Add all of the ingredients, except the absinthe, to a shaker tin; shake with ice until chilled.

2. Add a barspoon of absinthe to the chilled glass, roll the glass around to coat, then shake out any remaining absinthe.

3. Double-strain the cocktail into the glass. Express oil from a lemon peel over the top and garnish with the lemon twist (optional).

THE WOODS SPIRIT CO.

When I interviewed Fabio Martini of The Woods Spirit Co. years ago, he and partner Joel Myers were foragers whose idea to start a craft distillery was ignited when they were hiking in the woods. Back then, Martini said, "We started out wanting to make a gin from the forest." Something made them change course. BC was experiencing a Campari shortage (again), which meant the bitter orange standard-bearer wasn't accessible. So neither were Negronis.

It's old news now, but Martini and Myers' first focus for The Woods Spirit Co. was to create its flagship amaro. Later the distillery expanded its collection to include other Italian-style liqueurs like its nocino made from green walnuts, limoncello, and more.

The North Vancouver distillery is neighbors with Sons of Vancouver, which provided plenty of support to Martini and Myers when they were getting started and didn't yet have a place to distill their spirits. Now, visitors can kick back in the distillery's cocktail lounge and sip on (what else?) a Negroni made with The Woods' gin, barrel-aged amaro, and sweet vermouth, among other cocktail creations.

WINTER VAYCAY

THE WOODS SPIRIT CO., NORTH VANCOUVER

Bartender Robert Clough says the Winter Vacay is "a short, strong riff on a piña colada. Coconut and lots of juniper are the backbone, a little bitter character from Woods Chiaro, sweetened with fresh pineapple syrup, and lime juice to balance." Instead of reaching for the traditional rum, Clough chooses gin and fat-washes the spirit with coconut butter.

GLASSWARE: Nick & Nora glass

GARNISH: Dehydrated pineapple

- 1½ oz. (45 ml) Coconut-Butter-Washed The Woods Spirit Co. Gin (see recipe opposite)
- ¾ oz. (22.5 ml) The Woods Spirit Co. Chiaro Amaro
- ¾ oz. (22.5 ml) Pineapple Syrup (see recipe below)
- ½ oz. (15 ml) lime juice

1. Combine all of the ingredients in a shaker with ice.

2. Shake hard, then fine-strain the cocktail into the Nick & Nora glass.

PINEAPPLE SYRUP: Juice one whole ripe pineapple and measure. In a pot set over low heat, make a 2:1 rich simple syrup with white sugar and pineapple juice. Remove from heat once the sugar is dissolved and the citric acid is to taste.

COCONUT-BUTTER-WASHED THE WOODS SPIRIT CO. GIN: Liquify ¼ pound (115 grams) of coconut butter. Add one 25½ oz. (750 ml) bottle of The Woods Spirit Co. Gin, stir, and leave overnight in the refrigerator. The fat will separate from the alcohol and solidify on top. Pierce a hole in the solidified fat, fine-strain, and it's ready to use.

BARTENDER TIP: Alcohol does a good job of extracting flavors and textures from fat. This method will work using other fats (butter, bacon, etc.) and high-strength alcohol (rum/bourbon, etc.). For extra clarification, leave the strained alcohol in the refrigerator for 24 hours. The small particles will settle at the bottom of the alcohol, allowing you to strain off 95 percent of the residue, leaving a beautiful, clarified infusion.

BLACK MANHATTAN

THE WOODS SPIRIT CO., NORTH VANCOUVER

Green walnuts picked in Summerland go into this traditional northern Italy spirit inspired by a recipe from Fabio Martini's family. This Black Manhattan is "a complex twist on a classic," says bartender Robert Clough. "Calvados and bourbon make up the base providing apple, American, and French oak. The Woods Spirit Co. Nocino is rich, nutty, and sweet with winter spice."

GLASSWARE: Coupe glass
GARNISH: Luxardo cherry

- 1 oz. (30 ml) Calvados
- 1 oz. (30 ml) bourbon
- ¾ oz. (22.5 ml) The Woods Spirit Co. Nocino

1. Combine all of the ingredients in a mixing glass with ice.

2. Stir 20 times, then strain the cocktail into the coupe.

3. Garnish with the Luxardo cherry.

THE LIBERTY DISTILLERY

There's always a hive of activity at Granville Island, with its massive public market and artisans working inside the corrugated iron walls of their studios year-round. Smack in the middle sits The Liberty Distillery. Since opening in 2013, the distillery has been an anchor for the island, inviting curious patrons to tour its operations and sip a craft cocktail while sitting at its authentic 125-year-old bar.

With brand names such as Truth, Trust, and Endeavour, The Liberty Distillery has made its staunch support for traditional distilling methods and dedication to using 100 percent BC organic grain as crystal clear as its series of triple-distilled gins, vodkas, and unaged grain spirits. Look for unconventional spirits such as its Truth Oak Vodka (it won silver at the San Francisco World Spirits Competition in 2020), along with the distillery's selection of half a dozen types of whiskey.

LIBERTY'S NEW YORK SOUR

THE LIBERTY DISTILLERY, GRANVILLE ISLAND

This classic bourbon-based cocktail will test your technique with its signature float of red wine. Naturally, The Liberty Distillery shakes up this favorite with its own product, Trust Whiskey–Single Grain. The limited release spirit starts with organic hull-less unmalted barley and is aged for three years in ex-bourbon barrels. It was named Whisky of the Year–Alternative Grain, at the Canadian Whisky Awards 2023.

GLASSWARE: Rocks glass, chilled
GARNISH: Maraschino cherry on a pick

- 1½ oz. (45 ml) Trust Whiskey–Single Grain
- 1 oz. (15 ml) fresh lemon juice
- 1 oz. (15 ml) egg white
- ¾ oz. (22.5 ml) simple syrup
- ¼ oz. (7.5 ml) dry red wine

1. Chill a rocks glass. In a Boston shaker glass, add the whiskey, lemon juice, egg white, and simple syrup. Fill with ice and shake vigorously.

2. Strain into the chilled, ice-filled rocks glass.

3. Using the backside of a barspoon resting on the inside edge of the rocks glass, slowly pour the red wine to create a float.

4. Garnish with a skewered cherry on a pick.

LIBERTY'S BURGUNDY SUNSET

THE LIBERTY DISTILLERY, GRANVILLE ISLAND

In 2022, The Liberty Distillery's Trust Single Cask–Burgundy Whiskey took home two silver awards at the Canadian Artisan Spirit Competition and the Canadian Whisky Awards.

GLASSWARE: Collins glass, chilled

GARNISH: Orange peel twist skewered with a maraschino cherry

- 1½ oz. (45 ml) Trust Single Cask–Burgundy Whiskey
- ¾ oz. (22.5 ml) fresh lemon juice
- ½ oz. (15 ml) Frostbites Mango Passionfruit Cordial
- ¼ oz. (7.5 ml) Giffard Cassis Syrup

1. In a Boston shaker glass, add all of the ingredients, except the cassis syrup. Fill with ice and shake vigorously.

2. Pour the cassis syrup into the bottom of the chilled collins glass. Strain and pour the cocktail into the glass.

3. Garnish with the orange peel twist skewered with a maraschino cherry.

ODD SOCIETY SPIRITS

Odd Society Spirits in East Vancouver needs little introduction; you'll recognize the distillery's products in dozens of recipes throughout this book. Opened in 2013, the small-batch distillery is a family affair, its team led by founder and distiller Gordon Glanz, general manager Miriam Karp, and bar manager Mia Glanz, their daughter. Underpinning Odd Society's success is its marriage of old-world distilling methods and new-world ingredients that come together in exciting, experimental spirits and limited-release products, from its signature vodka and seasonal salal gin to liqueurs and whiskey.

And the innovation never seems to stop. In 2021, Odd Society released its inaugural Peat & Smoke series whiskey that uses peated malt from Washington State and Scotland to create a taste of the terroirs of those two regions. As expected, the ingenuity and innovation at Odd Society has translated into a slew of medals over the years. Its Peated Whisky, Prospector Rye Whisky, and Smoke and Peat each won silver at the 2023 Canadian Whisky Awards.

VIOLET & CLAIRE

ODD SOCIETY SPIRITS, EAST VANCOUVER

Mia Glanz's cocktail menu showcases spirits made in-house as they rotate seasonally. With an eye to sustainability, she uses waste products from the back-of-house operations to create bespoke syrups, bitters, infusions, liqueurs. Glanz says it's all about flavor and oddball ingredients.

Below, she pays homage to one of her favorite adolescent novels *Violet + Claire* (by Francesca Lia Block) about a pair of best friends with different dispositions, one blonde and the other brunette. This is the summer version of the cocktail. "The Violet + Claire has been on the menu at Odd Society for years," says Glanz, "but it's somewhat amorphous, with different seasonal iterations. The consistent aspect is its two-part structure, in two colors: a base and a boozy foam."

GLASSWARE: Coupe glass
GARNISH: Limoncello Foam (see recipe below)

- 1½ oz. (45 ml) Odd Society East Van Vodka
- 1½ oz. (45 ml) pineapple juice
- ½ oz. (15 ml) Odd Society Créme de Cassis
- ⅓ oz. (10 ml) fino sherry

1. In a shaker, shake all of the ingredients together with ice.

2. Fine-strain the cocktail into a coupe.

3. Garnish with the Limoncello Foam.

LIMONCELLO FOAM: In a mason jar, place 14 oz. limoncello (415 ml), 8 egg whites, 2 cups (500 ml) whipped cream, 2 barspoons citric acid, and 12 dashes Ms. Better's Pineapple Star Anise Bitters. Shake to combine. Chill the foam in the refrigerator. Charge in a whipped cream canister before using.

LONG TABLE DISTILLERY

When Long Table Distillery kicked off operations in 2013, owners Charles and Rita Tremewen were firmly focused on making gin, earning the independent distillery an armload of accolades at events such as the San Francisco World Spirits Competition. In each batch is 100 percent Canadian grain alcohol as well as organic ingredients and locally foraged botanicals. Long Table's portfolio extended to its small-batch vodka, which employs unique elements such as limestone from Texada Island on the Sunshine Coast, and its signature Långbord Akvavit that follows a traditional Scandinavian recipe.

In summer 2022, the Tremewens passed the torch to Simon and Kimberley Brown. "We're both originally from the UK," says Simon, "and gin is in our blood." Inspired by operations at a distillery in Bath, the Browns recently launched cocktail-making classes to let guests try their hands at mixing drinks with Long Table's spirits mere steps from where they're made. Brown shares a trio of recipes that show off the distillery's diversity of spirits in interesting and approachable ways.

ELDER FASHION

LONG TABLE DISTILLERY, DOWNTOWN

The Elder Fashion is a riff on the classic Old Fashioned but brings together Long Table's barrel-aged gin, which earned bronze at the San Francisco World Spirits Competition in 2015, and elderflower liqueur.

GLASSWARE: Old-fashioned glass
GARNISH: Orange slice or rind

- 1¾ oz. (52.5 ml) Long Table Barrel-Aged Gin
- ¼ oz. (7.5 ml) St-Germain Elderflower Liqueur
- 1 sugar cube
- Orange bitters, to taste

1. In a dry stirring glass, muddle together the sugar cube and orange bitters. Add the gin and elderflower liqueur.

2. Pour the cocktail into an old-fashioned glass over one large ice cube.

3. Garnish with a slice of orange or orange rind.

ESPRESSO MARTINI CANADIANA

LONG TABLE DISTILLERY, DOWNTOWN

Dick Bradsell's modern classic from the 1983 has made a come-back. Long Table's version adds a touch of maple syrup to the Espresso Martini to create a Canadian take on the original.

GLASSWARE: Martini glass

GARNISH: Coffee beans, Pocky stick

- 1½ oz. (45 ml) Long Table Texada Vodka
- 1 oz. (30 ml) espresso
- ½ oz. (15 ml) coffee liquor
- ½ oz. (15 ml) maple syrup
- 2 dashes chocolate bitters

1. In a Boston shaker, dry-shake (no ice) all of the ingredients.

2. Add ice and wet-shake.

3. Strain the cocktail into the martini glass and garnish with three coffee beans and a Pocky stick.

KARDEMUMMA

LONG TABLE DISTILLERY, DOWNTOWN

Long Table's Långbord Akvavit can be sipped neat as an aperitif or digestif. Below, Brown uses it to craft a sour with licorice notes.

GLASSWARE: Stemless wine glass or rocks glass
GARNISH: Dehydrated grapefruit, shaved cinnamon

- 2 oz. (60 ml) Long Table Långbord Akvavit
- 1 oz. (30 ml) fresh lemon juice
- ¾ oz. (22.5 ml) Rich Cardamom Syrup (see recipe below)

- House-made orange bitters
- Egg white or vegan foamer

1. In a shaker, shake all of the ingredients with ice.

2. Fine-strain the cocktail through a mesh strainer into the glass and garnish with the dehydrated grapefruit and a shaving of fresh cinnamon.

RICH CARDAMOM SYRUP: In a hot pan, lightly toast 1 whole cardamom seed. Add the rind of 1 whole lemon, 1 cinnamon stick, 1½ cups (350 ml) sugar, and 1 cup (250 ml) water. Bring to a boil and let it simmer for 4 to 6 minutes. Cool before using.

COPPERPENNY GIN & STORMY

COPPERPENNY DISTILLING CO, NORTH VANCOUVER

Like most people who live in North Vancouver, Jan Stenc is highly attuned to the weather. But not necessarily for the reasons you might expect. Storm systems like the benignly named Pineapple Express have had an interesting impact on the distilling operations Stenc runs with his wife, Jennifer Kom-Tong, at The Shipyards in North Vancouver. When tropical jet streams, often from Hawaii, drive moisture-laden clouds into the mountains, the clouds dump massive amounts of rain on North Shore residents (Stenc says they get eighty more rain days per year than the rest of Metro Vancouver across the water, a couple kilometers south).

But Stenc sees a silver lining in all those clouds. "It is this very water—clean, sweet, and plentiful mountain water—that Copperpenny relies on to craft our small-batch gins and liqueurs," he says. Plus it creates a little drama, something he and Kom-Tong are comfortable with. The couple are longtime set designers for the film industry and took a deep dive into distilling when they opened Copperpenny in 2022, creating products such as a dry gin and their own style of orange liqueur called Just a Sec. The cocktail lounge has become a glam gathering place to enjoy live music from local acts and retreat from the ever-present rain.

"In this summery cocktail, Copperpenny Gin No. 005 delivers uniquely bright citrus notes from fresh Californian orange peel and a blend of Canadian and Egyptian coriander, a little-discussed botanical critical to the flavor character of most gins," says Stenc. "This punchy, citrusy combo pairs well with the vibrant tropical sweetness of freshly pressed Hawaiian pineapple juice, a fruit that is readily available year-round in Vancouver."

GARNISH: Ground sumac and raw cane sugar rim, pineapple wedge

- 2 oz. (60 ml) Copperpenny Gin No. 005
- 2 oz. (60 ml) slow-pressed Hawaiian pineapple juice
- ½ oz. (15 ml) freshly-squeezed lime juice
- Fever-Tree Ginger Beer, to top

1. Rim a collins glass with a 1:1 mixture of ground sumac and raw cane sugar. Fill the glass with cubed ice.

2. Add all of the ingredients into the glass. Top with the ginger beer until full.

3. Stir lightly and garnish with the pineapple wedge.

GIN & TONIC

YALETOWN DISTILLING COMPANY, YALETOWN

The Yaletown Distilling Company has been a fixture in Vancouver's former warehouse district since it opened its doors on December 5, 2013, the anniversary of Repeal Day in the United States. At the time of writing, the distillery had just changed ownership. It will continue to make gin and vodka, as well as host tours of its operations, says Yaletown's head distiller Denton Meyer, who worked at the Eau Claire Distillery in Alberta before moving west. "I like to use a lot of citrus, dried lemon, and orange . . . BC kelp to get the saltiness of the citrus." Meyer keeps it simple with this classic Gin & Tonic recipe that lets the spirit's botanicals shine.

GLASSWARE: Rocks glass

- 2 oz. (60 ml) Yaletown Distilling Company Gin
- Fever-Tree Tonic Water, to top

1. Pour the gin into a rocks glass with ice.

2. Fill with the tonic water.

CANADIAN
ALCOHOLOMETRIC
TABLES

TABLES
ALCOOMÉTRIQUES
CANADIENNES

1980

MEET THE MAKERS

Exploring a distillery's operations is an ideal way to meet the minds and makers behind the spirts and learn about the art and science that go into creating craft spirits. How should you prepare? What should you expect? Charlene Rooke, lead judge of the Canadian Artisan Spirits Competition (and an expert on BC spirits) offers tips on how to get the most out of your experience, and how to sample the spirits whether you're at a distillery, bar, or at home.

Stay hydrated: This is not the time for pregaming or the place for getting drunk, says Rooke. Show up hydrated and with a full stomach.

Hands off: It's easy to be dazzled by copper columns and pot stills but resist the temptation to touch. "A distillery is a manufacturing plant," says Rooke. "It's a safe environment, but technically, it's explosive. Don't touch the stills and try to stay out of the way."

Mind your manners: "These craft distillers are serious badasses. They may seem very modest on the surface, but trust me, they know more than you do." Rooke says it's not the time to show off if you've been to Kentucky or Scotland or talk about bottles you've tasted. This is the moment for the distillery staff to shine.

Be open-minded: "Give craft spirits a chance," says Rooke. "Some can be a little bit funky, but that's why you seek these things out. If you go to a craft distillery and taste something local and handmade with a sense of place, it's going have some flavor. And that includes vodka, gin, whiskey . . . just about anything you might be tasting if you're comparing it in your mind and palate to a commercial spirit." Rooke adds that it's unfair to compare a craft spirit to one that's been made for decades or centuries. There's a spectrum of quality and style, all of which deserves respect.

Slow down: If sampling spirits is part of your distillery tour, take it slow. It's about sniffing, sipping, and savoring (see below). You're not doing shots. It's a chance to learn. Every distillery is unique, and you'll come away learning a bit more about how each place operates.

Share the wealth: The good stuff is expensive, as it should be, says Rooke. "It's not very polite to go into a craft distillery where someone is producing an artisan spirit and mention that it's double the cost of something at the liquor store." Tip after your tour, and if you enjoyed the spirits you tasted, buy a bottle on the spot to support local distillers.

Tasting 101

Use your senses: When sampling a straight spirit, there are three things to consider: appearance, nose, and palate—color, aroma, and flavors.

1. Color won't tell you much about a spirit. Sometimes it's an indication of age, but in many parts of the world (but not for BC craft distilling!), it's legal to add artificial coloring.

2. Don't swirl the spirit in the glass like you would with wine; that stirs up the ethanol and can burn out your nose and palate. If you want, give it a slow roll to coat the glass and let the ethanol dissipate. Take a gentle sniff (use both nostrils) and keep your mouth open while you inhale. "We all know that taste is mostly smell," says Rooke. "We really only taste sweet, sour, salty, bitter, and umami, but the nose can detect millions of smells.

3. Likewise, after swallowing the spirit, breathe in through your mouth and then out through your nose. You'll get a huge burst of flavor on your palate. That's called retro nasal breathing, harnessing the power of the nose and the palate together. And have some water on the side. "Adding a little water really enhances the aromas and flavors. Take your time and let it open up. If you sip on that spirit and come back to it in 10 minutes, if it's a well-made spirit, particularly whiskey, it will totally change and open up and bloom in the glass."

PEGU CLUB IN THE WOODS

MS. BETTER'S BITTERS

It might seem audacious to use the word "miraculous" in your signature products, but Ms. Better's can back it up. (This book alone has plenty of endorsements.) In 2017, Ms. Better's Bitters publicly launched, thanks in part to the buzz created by its Miraculous Foamer, the first product of its kind worldwide. The botanical egg white substitute is shelf stable, allergen free, compact, and water soluble. It's vegan-friendly, and has even been endorsed by PETA.

Phil and Sam Unger are the father–daughter team behind Ms. Better's Bitters. He's a food scientist. She's a perfumer. They've worked together for years, with Sam doing brand development and flavor creation with her father. Ms. Better's Bitters is made exclusively in Vancouver and distributed in more than twenty countries.

Tarquin Melnyk has been a bartender for almost two decades. When he was running Gastown bar Bambudda with Dylan Williams, he met Sam and Phil. Eventually the four teamed up, with Melnyk assisting with product research and development. Melnyk's Pegu Club in the Woods is a riff on the classic that uses a regional botanical bitter called Cypress Bowl. "These bitters have fresh alpine flavors and woodsy texture, all sourced from the Cypress Bowl mountain range to the immediate north of Vancouver," says Melnyk. "This 'maritime rainforest' is an abundant growing zone, and these bitters are like walking its trails." He says there's a perfect synergy in pairing the grapefruit bitters with the grand fir in the Cypress Bowl.

BETTER WITH BITTERS

Cocktail bitters are a bar staple that can help balance and accentuate flavors in a drink or add a whole new layer of complexity. They're highly concentrated flavor bombs made by infusing alcohol with ingredients such as orange peel, spices, and gentian root, among myriad others. Typically, only a dash or two are required to bring their essence to a cocktail.

GLASSWARE: Coupe glass, chilled

GARNISH: Fresh lime peel

- 2 oz. (60 ml) Copperpenny Distilling Co Dry Gin
- 1 oz. (30 ml) fresh lime juice
- ¾ oz. (22.5 ml) Copperpenny Distilling Co Just A Sec
- 2 dashes Ms. Better's Cypress Bowl Bitters
- 1 dash Ms. Better's Grapefruit Bitters

1. Pour all of the ingredients into a cocktail shaker. Add ice and shake vigorously.

2. Fine-strain the cocktail into the chilled coupe.

3. Garnish with the fresh lime peel.

ARTISANAL ICE

Jay Browne knows his way around a bar and what it takes to make stellar cocktails. The twenty-year industry veteran was looking for a new venture that would allow him to avoid long nights and spend more time with his young family, while still keeping in touch with his bartender brethren. Originally from the UK, Browne honed his skills at bars in London, arriving in Vancouver in 2009. Here, he crafted cocktails at Bao Bei, and the Calabash Dark and Stormy at the Caribbean bistro in Gastown, which stocks more than eighty types of rum.

"I'm half Japanese, half English," says Browne, who had originally considered opening an establishment that embraced the best of both countries' pub cultures, along with Japanese techniques. "I wanted to have large blocks of ice on the bar that I would cut down into workable types of ice for service," he says. "There's a lot to be said for that type of bartending, and a lot of it comes down to finesse and perfection and economy of movement and real showmanship."

On a trip to New York around 2009, Browne visited Milk & Honey, which was helmed by Sasha Petraske, who was freezing ice in a hotel pan overnight to create big blocks for cocktails. "They were spending three hours prep before service to cut this stuff down into big chunks that were going into the glass. At that time, it was just purely aesthetic."

Browne wanted to create that same artisanal quality and make it accessible to

bars around Vancouver. Kodama Ice Co currently crafts a dozen dimensions of ice, from square cubes to rectangles, and spears that are ideal for collins glasses. The ice is ultra-clear, adding another element to a cocktail. It's also super-compressed so it melts slower, allowing the bartender to have more control over how quickly the drink is diluted.

Kodama uses Vancouver tap water, along with industrial filters to remove chlorine and other impurities. "The machines we use make 300-pound blocks of ice. You have to use an engine hoist to pick these up," says Browne. "We break them down with chainsaws, and we have a very large industrial saw that moves horizontally; it's basically been adapted from cutting trees into slabs. Then we cut those down into cubes." Ice is often an overlooked yet essential ingredient that elevates the sipping experience.

HYPER-LOCAL SIPPING

COUNCIL OF TREES

MARIGOLD'S GIMLET

HOTEL GEORGIA

LADY WALLFLOWER

WEREWOLF IN VANCOUVER

MUSH BE LOVE

HONEY CRUSHED LEMONADE

BRITISH COLUMBIA OLD FASHIONED

LA ROUGE

ARCTIC MISTRESS

21ST NIGHT

THE RICKSHAW

BLACK HEART MANHATTAN

EMPRESS MARTINI

Wherever you wander in Vancouver, it's hard not to be seduced by the city's natural surroundings. Lush forests beckon with the scent of cedars and salal berries suspended between waxy green leaves. With the right knowledge, mushrooms can be foraged safely, and wild blackberries are easy to come by, even along urban alleys.

Bartenders are not afraid to take inspiration from our environs, whether guided by the seasons, terroir, or pride of place. Some reach for flora such as marigolds for a Gimlet. Others forage for moss to mix with cedar chips in a syrup. And many are crafting their cocktails with internationally acclaimed spirits distilled close to home. They are pushing boundaries while pressing these products into service, not solely to be loyal to local but also to embody deeply held ethics like dedication to sustainable sources and plant-based products.

All these cocktails are an homage to the city in some way, even the eponymous Hotel Georgia cocktail, whose creator might have introduced the world to the dry shake.

COUNCIL OF TREES

BOTANIST BAR, FAIRMONT PACIFIC RIM

There's always been some alchemy at Botanist Bar in the Fairmont Pacific Rim Hotel. A mysterious cocktail lab lends itself to experimentation with items like a centrifuge. But there's no magic in the machines without the creative minds and skillful hands of experts such as head bartender Jeff Savage. He could fill a full page with accolades. As part of the Botanist team, Savage helped nab the 2022 Michelin Guide Vancouver Exceptional Cocktails Award, and second place in Canada's 50 Best Bars rankings the same year.

Prior to the pandemic, Savage was named Diageo World Class Canada Bartender of the Year 2019 (followed by a second-place finish in the international finals). He and the Botanist team also won the 2019 Bols Around the World global bartending competition. So, when you walk up the marble steps from the hotel lobby into Botanist Bar, prepare to have your mind pried open—wide open. The Council of Trees cocktail is a hint of what you can expect.

It starts with the cryptic notions printed beneath its description: "Conversations seemingly unspoken in languages completely unknown still determine much more than we know." The cipher sounds like a reference to UBC forester Suzanne Simard and Stanley Park, the 1,001-acre sanctuary in the city, teeming with ancient conifers just over a mile away.

In this whiskey-meets-woods concoction, Savage notes that both sherry and Scotch are aged in oak. Then he layers in local elements like foraged oak moss and birch water (from the heart of the tree), along with tea leaves smoked in Vancouver with alder and cherry wood (and sometimes oak staves from whiskey casks). It all concentrates the essence of a forest in a glass. If at first you didn't believe trees could talk, after one sip of this cocktail, you'll realize they speak volumes without ever saying a word.

GLASSWARE: Collins glass

GARNISH: Fresh amaranth flower

- 1½ oz. (45 ml) birch water
- 1 oz. (30 ml) Johnnie Walker Black
- ¾ oz. (22.5 ml) Smoked Tea Syrup (see recipe at right)
- ½ oz. (15 ml) fino sherry
- ¼ oz. (7.5 ml) Oak Moss Syrup (see recipe at right)

1. Combine all of the ingredients in a stirring vessel; stir with ice until chilled and diluted.

2. Strain the cocktail into a collins glass with fresh ice.

3. Botanist Bar garnishes this drink with a fresh amaranth flower, but a rosemary sprig will work perfectly in a pinch.

SMOKED TEA SYRUP: In a pan, combine ¼ cup (50 grams) food-grade western red cedar chips, 4½ teaspoons (20 grams) smoked tea (Botanist uses Tealeaves' BC Forestea, but any smoked tea should work), and 4¼ cups (1,000 ml) water. Simmer over medium heat. Let the mixture steep with the lid on for 20 minutes. Strain the liquid. Add 4¼ cups (1,000 grams) sugar and ½ cup (100 grams) citric acid to the mix. Stir well to combine. Let the syrup chill and store it in a sealed container for up to 1 month in the refrigerator.

OAK MOSS SYRUP: Soak 3 tablespoons (40 grams) dried oak moss* in boiled water for 20 minutes. Strain and dump the water, keeping the hydrated oak moss. Add the oak moss and 4½ teaspoons (20 grams) cedar chips to water in a pot over low heat. Bring to a very low simmer for 20 minutes. Strain out the solids. To the liquid portion, add 4¼ cups (1 kilogram) sugar and stir until the sugar is dissolved. Let the syrup chill and store it in a sealed container for up to 1 month in the refrigerator.

MARIGOLD'S GIMLET

BURDOCK & CO, MOUNT PLEASANT

Burdock & Co is another one of Vancouver's beloved restaurants that lets the spotlight shine brightly on local ingredients and the stewardship of farmers and foragers. But in 2022, the attention was fully focused on the team led by chef and owner Andrea Carlson when Michelin awarded it a star for its farm-to-table cuisine.

That same deft hand and dedication extend to Burdock & Co's drinks. "This cocktail is a fresh botanical take on a Gimlet using local ingredients, like gin from Victoria on Vancouver Island and sake from Artisan SakeMaker on Granville Island in Vancouver," says Carlson. "The marigold is a workhorse of a flower; farmers often plant it between rows for pest control. It imparts a very lovely fragrance here and a deep body to the cocktail."

GLASSWARE: Vintage coupe glass
GARNISH: Marigold petals

- 1 oz. (30 ml) Victoria Gin
- 1 oz. (30 ml) Artisan SakeMaker Osake Junmai Nama Sake
- 1 oz. (30 ml) Marigold

Flower Syrup (see recipe at right)
- ¾ oz. (22.5 ml) lime juice
- 2 dashes Bittered Sling Orange & Juniper Bitters

1. Combine the gin, sake, Marigold Flower Syrup, lime juice, and bitters in a cocktail shaker.

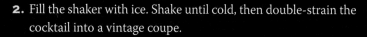

2. Fill the shaker with ice. Shake until cold, then double-strain the cocktail into a vintage coupe.

3. Garnish with the marigold petals.

MARIGOLD FLOWER SYRUP: In a small pot, combine 1 cup (250 ml) water and 1 cup (250 ml) sugar. Bring to a simmer, add 10 marigold flowers (any color), and turn the heat to low. Gently steep the syrup over heat for 30 to 45 minutes. Strain. The syrup can be stored in the refrigerator for 7 to 10 days.

THE SCIENCE OF THE SHAKE

Shaking a cocktail involves skill, style, and a little science. When a bartender agitates ingredients, there's more going on than meets the eye. The key purpose is to combine ingredients and chill and dilute the cocktail.

Recipes like sours and fizzes that incorporate egg whites (or vegan alternatives) sometimes call for a two-shake method. First is the "dry shake," without ice, to whip air into the egg whites, creating a fluffy foam. Next, ice is added for a "wet shake" that quickly cools the cocktail before it's strained into a chilled glass. As sharp-eyed cocktail aficionados have noted, Saucier might have pioneered the dry shake—or at least he was the first to put his instructions in print. It was, in fact, in reference to the Hotel Georgia cocktail. Saucier writes: "Shake well before adding ice. This gives a nice 'top.' Then add ice to chill and serve in a cocktail glass."

Some bartenders believe that shaking egg whites with ice inhibits a meringue-like foam from forming. Thus, the reverse dry shake: wet-shake first with ice but no egg whites; then strain out the ice, add the egg whites, and shake again. Pour into a chilled glass (straining a second time, if desired).

Stephen Sherry, bar manager at Gastronomy Gastown (see page 89)

HOTEL GEORGIA

Grandeur and glamor are watchwords for the Rosewood Hotel Georgia, which opened in 1927. During the decades following, the five-star luxury property has played host to the glitterati from Elvis Presley and Nat "King" Cole to Katharine Hepburn and British royalty. Since then, it has served up both classic and modern cocktails to discerning guests and locals alike. Brad Stanton, original bar manager at Hawksworth Bar, adapted the hotel's namesake cocktail (reducing the orgeat) from a recipe first found in print in Ted Saucier's 1951 book, *Bottoms Up*.

◆

GLASSWARE: Coupe glass, chilled
GARNISH: Freshly grated nutmeg

- 1½ oz. (45 ml) Beefeater Gin
- 1 oz. (30 ml) lemon juice
- ½ oz. (15 ml) orgeat syrup
- 1 egg white
- 4 dashes orange blossom water

1. Add all of the ingredients, except the nutmeg, to a shaker.

2. Shake with ice (wet-shake) until well chilled.

3. Strain to remove the ice. Shake without ice (dry-shake) to whip air into the egg white.

4. Strain the cocktail into the chilled coupe. Garnish with grated nutmeg.

LADY WALLFLOWER

THE MACKENZIE ROOM, RAILTOWN

We have a dish on our menu called the Showstopper Salad," says Alexia David, beverage director at The Mackenzie Room. "It's been on the menu since day one," she adds. "I like to say this cocktail is the equivalent of that salad. Quite often, I joke that I'll die before this cocktail does." The Railtown restaurant has a rustic-meets-refined atmosphere with about a dozen seats at the bar for dining and drinking cocktails like the Lady Wallflower created by Arthur Wynne gets its name in reference to edible flowers and the Odd Society Wallflower Gin.

David recommends this gateway drink to guests who are still discovering the world of cocktails. "It's equal parts refreshing, rich, complex, and pretty. Bonus points: the liquor elements of this drink come from Odd Society Spirits, which just so happens to be down the road from The Mackenzie Room. Support your friends and neighbors!"

GLASSWARE: Coupe glass
GARNISH: Seasonal edible flowers or drops of cassis

- 1½ oz. (45 ml) Odd Society Wallflower Gin
- ½ oz. (15 ml) Odd Society Crème de Cassis
- ½ oz. (15 ml) simple syrup (1:1)
- 1 oz. (30 ml) lime juice
- 1 oz. (30 ml) or 1 egg white
- 1 dash Bittered Sling Plum & Rootbeer Bitters

1. Pour the gin and crème de cassis into a shaker. Add the lime juice and egg white.

2. Dry-shake for 30 seconds.

3. Add ice. Shake another 30 seconds.

4. Double-strain the cocktail into the coupe.

5. Garnish with edible flowers or drops of cassis.

WEREWOLF IN VANCOUVER

THE MACKENZIE ROOM, EAST VANCOUVER

Alexia David describes this cocktail, which also uses local spirits and bitters as "a sweeter, spicier, nuttier play on an Old Fashioned." For his recipe, Arthur Wynne might be tempting a transformation from human to mythical beast with this 100 proof spirit made from 100 percent rye. A hit of maple syrup balances the splash of chili water.

GLASSWARE: Smallish rocks glass

GARNISH: Castelvetrano olive wrapped in an orange swath

- 1¾ oz. (52.5 ml) Odd Society Mongrel Unaged Spirit
- ½ oz. (15 ml) maple syrup
- ⅓ oz. (10 ml) Chili Water (see recipe below)
- 1 teaspoon (5 ml) Bittered Sling Moondog Latin Bitters
- 20 drops (1 ml) Citric Acid Water (see recipe below)
- 20 drops (1 ml) Fee Brothers Black Walnut Bitters

1. Place all of the ingredients in a mixing glass over ice. Stir for about 30 seconds, or for an amount of time you feel is right.

2. Add 2 or 3 cubes of ice to the rocks glass. Pour the cocktail over ice into the glass.

3. Garnish with a Castelvetrano olive wrapped with an orange peel.

CHILY WATER: Boil 3 cups (750 ml) of water and bring it down to a simmer. Once it's boiled, transfer the water to a container. Using a measuring cup, measure 1 cup (250 ml) of red chili pepper flakes and add it to water. Let the mixture steep for 24 hours. Strain out the chili flakes before use.

CITRIC ACID WATER: Dilute 1 heaping teaspoon (about 7 ml) of citric acid in about ³⁄₁₀ cup (100 ml) of boiling water. Allow the water to cool completely before use.

MUSH BE LOVE

THE ACORN, RILEY PARK

At the Acorn, a plant-driven restaurant in Riley Park, cocktails are often an ode to ingredients prepared with passion from seed to stem. That extends from the zero-waste kitchen through to the cocktails. "Mush Be Love is a tribute to mushroom lovers," says Shira Blustein, founder and general manager. "This cocktail represents the amazing ecosystem of the Pacific Northwest, specifically Vancouver's rainforests. It also strongly represents what we do at Acorn: working with locally grown and foraged seasonal plants as well as local purveyors and makers."

To create this cocktail, bartender Thiago Alves marries sweet and savory, starting with a 100 percent rye single-malt infused with local porcini and candy cap mushrooms. (It's the product of a community collab between Wild Thing Snack Bar and Odd Society Spirits.) Among other ingredients, he adds a touch of house-made caramel hit with maple-smoked sea salt harvested on Vancouver Island.

"Rich and creamy, this cocktail is suitable for dessert and would make the perfect nightcap," says Blustein. She adds that the delicious and festive flavors of Mush Be Love could easily stand up against the traditional eggnog during the holidays.

- 1 oz. (30 ml) Odd Society Mushroom Single Malt Whisky
- 1 oz. (30 ml) Madeira
- 1 oz. (30 ml) Baileys
- ¾ oz. (22.5 ml) egg white
- 1 barspoon Maple-Smoked Salted Caramel (see recipe below)
- 4 drops Amaretto-Coffee Tincture (see recipe at right)
- Larch and Dehydrated Candy Cap Mushroom Dust (see recipe at right)

1. In a cocktail shaker, combine the whiskey, Madeira, Baileys, egg white, and Maple-Smoked Salted Caramel.

2. Dry-shake (no ice) for 10 seconds to build up foam. Fill the shaker with ice and hard-shake.

3. Double-strain the cocktail into a short old-fashioned glass or coupe.

4. Heavily dust half the top of the glass with the Larch and Dehydrated Candy Cap Mushroom Dust (or cinnamon if you don't have it).

5. Add the Amaretto Coffee Tincture to the other half of the glass.

MAPLE-SMOKED SALTED CARAMEL: In a medium to large saucier pan, add 1 cup (200 grams) granulated sugar. Cook over medium-low heat until the sugar is completely dissolved, approximately 5 minutes. Add ½ cup (90 grams) of butter; let it melt. Turn the heat up to medium. Allow the ingredients to boil without mixing or whisking. If needed, you can occasionally gently stir or tip the pan from side to side to help things cook evenly and prevent burning at the bottom of the pan. Once the mixture turns a deep golden copper color, about 10 minutes, remove it from heat.

Immediately add 4¼ oz. (120 ml) of heavy whipping cream in a slow, steady stream, whisking as you go. The caramel will bubble up quite a bit, so be careful with this step: you don't want to get burned! Continue to whisk the caramel until well combined. Add 1 barspoon of Maple-Smoked Sea Salt Flakes (from Vancouver Island Sea Salt) and stir to combine. Let cool.

AMARETTO COFFEE TINCTURE: Add 2 tablespoons (30 grams) medium-roast coffee beans to 3½ oz. (100 ml) of high-proof vodka (70 percent or more) or neutral-grain spirit. Cover the mixture and infuse at room temperature for 48 hours. Strain the tincture into a small, resealable glass bottle. Add 1½ oz. (50 ml) Sons of Vancouver No. 82 Amaretto.

LARCH AND DEHYDRATED CANDY CAP MUSHROOM DUST: Add 2 tablespoons (30 grams) dried larch needles and 1½ tablespoons (20 grams) dried candy cap mushrooms to a blender or spice grinder. Blend until it becomes a fine powder.

HONEY CRUSHED LEMONADE

THE LIBERTY DISTILLERY, GRANVILLE ISLAND

Simple and superb are two words to describe this refreshing recipe that uses hyper-local ingredients like unaged whiskey infused with wildflower honey from the Chilliwack Valley, which lies south of Vancouver. The whiskey, distilled with 100 percent organic BC-grown barley, earned silver at the San Francisco World Spirits Competition in 2017.

GLASSWARE: Irish whiskey mug

GARNISH: Raspberry on a bamboo skewer, fresh mint sprig

- 2 fresh blackberries (and/or other berries)
- 1 oz. (30 ml) Railspur No. 2 Wildflower Honey Unaged Whiskey
- 2 fresh mint leaves
- ½ oz. (15 ml) Honey Syrup (see recipe at right)
- Fresh-Squeezed Lemonade Syrup (see recipe at right), to top

1. In a Boston shaker glass, add the berries and muddle them.

2. Add the whiskey, fresh mint, honey syrup, and some ice.

3. Fill the glass completely with ice, shake, and strain the cocktail into an ice-filled Irish whiskey mug.

4. Top with Fresh-Squeezed Lemonade Syrup. Garnish with the skewered raspberry and mint sprig.

HONEY SYRUP: Mix together 1 cup (200 grams) wildflower honey and 1 cup (250 ml) boiling water and stir well. Let the mixture sit for a minute, then funnel it into a squeeze bottle. Label and date the bottle.

FRESH-SQUEEZED LEMONADE SYRUP: First make a simple syrup by mixing 1 cup (200 grams) granulated sugar with 1 cup (250 ml) boiling water and stirring well. Once the simple syrup is cool, mix together 1 part simple syrup, 2 parts fresh lemon juice, and 2 parts cold water. Stir well. Label and date the bottle.

BRITISH COLUMBIA OLD FASHIONED

BARTHOLOMEW BAR, YALETOWN

The British Columbia Old Fashioned, crafted with Golden Grahams–infused local rye whiskey, gives new meaning to the term "cereal grains." It might be tempting to make this cocktail your breakfast of champions, but it's probably better to savor it in the evening. A cordial made with spiced apple ciders amps up the soothing appeal to this inventive take on a classic.

GLASSWARE: Old-fashioned glass

GARNISH: Toasted marshmallow, Golden Grahams

- 2 oz. (60 ml) Golden Grahams–Infused Odd Society Prospector Rye Whisky (see recipe below)
- ¼ oz. (7.5 ml) Spiced Apple Cider Cordial (see recipe at right)
- 3 dashes Ms. Better's Chocolate Bitters

1. Combine all of the ingredients in a mixing beaker and stir for 10 seconds.

2. Strain the cocktail into the old-fashioned glass over a large ice cube.

3. Garnish with Golden Grahams cereal and a toasted marshmallow.

GOLDEN GRAHAMS–INFUSED ODD SOCIETY PROSPECTOR RYE WHISKY: Mix a 25½ oz. (750 ml) bottle of Odd Society Prospector Rye Whisky with ⅓ cup (75 grams) Golden Grahams cereal. Leave to infuse for 24 hours, then strain using an oil filter.

SPICED APPLE CIDER CORDIAL: In a pot, place 2 cups (500 ml) apple juice, 1 can or 2 cups (500 ml) medium-dry cider, 2 lemons (halved), 4 whole star anise, 4 cinnamon sticks, and 20 cloves. Bring the mixture to a boil. Lower the heat and let it simmer for 10 minutes, then add 2¼ cups (500 grams) sugar. Once the sugar is dissolved, strain the cordial and store.

LA ROUGE

THE LIBERTY DISTILLERY, GRANVILLE ISLAND

If you skim the recipe for La Rouge, it becomes apparent the cocktail is a hyper-local riff on the Bramble, a modern classic invented by London bartender Dick Bradsell in the 1980s. The Liberty Distillery's Endeavour Origins Gin is distilled with 100 percent organic BC wheat and more than two dozen handpicked wild BC botanicals that capture the distinctive flavors of the West Coast. (The gin won gold for Excellence in Terroir at the 2021 and 2022 Canadian Artisan Spirit Competition.) Unlike the original Bramble, this version is a little less boozy, using blackberry syrup instead of liqueur and an unexpected hit of heat from a habanero-based tincture.

GLASSWARE: Martini glass, chilled

GARNISH: Fresh blackberry on a bamboo skewer

- 1½ oz. (45 ml) Endeavour Origins Gin
- 1½ oz. (45 ml) Giffard Blackberry Syrup
- ½ oz. (15 ml) fresh lemon juice
- 3 dashes Scrappy's Firewater Tincture

1. In a shaker glass, add all of the ingredients, fill with ice, and shake vigorously.

2. Strain the cocktail into the chilled martini glass. Garnish with the fresh blackberry on a bamboo skewer.

ARCTIC MISTRESS

MILA, CHINATOWN

Plants and the planet are the focus of ethical and sustainable dining at MILA, a new addition to Chinatown's robust restaurant scene. When chef Breanne Smart needed a cocktail to round out the restaurant's holiday menu, she came up with the Arctic Mistress. Following the restaurant's new tradition, the cocktail was named in honor of a song by Canadian artist Les Stroud.

For this cocktail, Smart sought to recreate the flavors of a holiday dinner, infusing rosemary and thyme in vodka. "We've partnered with Indigenous World Winery and Spirits for years," she says, referring to BC's only 100 percent Indigenous-owned business of its kind, which embraces traditional Syilx culture with modern methods. To keep the cocktail vegan, Smart uses Ms. Better's Bitters Miraculous Foamer. "It's a bartender's best friend and fantastic alternative to using egg white to foam up a cocktail." The Arctic Mistress has quickly become a favorite cocktail for MILA's guests.

GLASSWARE: Coupe glass

GARNISH: Dehydrated granny smith apple slice

- **10 drops (½ pipette) Ms. Better's Bitters Miraculous Foamer**
- **1 oz. (30 ml) Rosemary and Thyme–Infused Indigenous World Spirits Vodka (see recipe below)**
- **1 oz. (30 ml) Berentzen Apple Liqueur**
- **½ oz. (15 ml) Apple-Rhubarb Syrup (see recipe at right)**
- **¼ oz. (7.5 ml) lemon juice**

1. Place the foamer in a shaker cup and shake vigorously for 30 seconds until the liquid turns into foam.

2. Add all of the other ingredients and ½ cup (125 ml) of ice. Shake well, until the outside of the shaker frosts up to the top.

3. Strain the cocktail into the coupe.

4. Garnish with the dehydrated apple slice.

ROSEMARY AND THYME–INFUSED INDIGENOUS WORLD SPIRITS VODKA: Add 1 tablespoon (15 ml) dried rosemary and 1 tablespoon (15 ml) dried thyme to 16 oz. (500 ml) of Indigenous World Spirits Vodka. Seal the mixture in a container and allow it to infuse for 24 hours. Remove the herbs. If you prefer a much earthier, stronger herb flavor, feel free to infuse for longer.

APPLE-RHUBARB SYRUP: In a pot over medium-high heat, combine 2.6 oz. (75 grams) apples (cored and sliced), 2.6 oz. (75 grams) frozen rhubarb, 1 cup (225 grams) water, and 1 cup (225 grams) cane sugar. Bring the mixture to a boil, reduce heat, and cook on low for 20 minutes. Remove the syrup from heat and let it cool and infuse for 30 minutes. Strain out the fruit and refrigerate.

21ST NIGHT

MILA, CHINATOWN

MILA bartender Jessie Abbott created the 21st Night as a September send-off to a long and memorable Vancouver summer. A lover of margaritas, Abbott was inspired by their extensive travels to Mexico to craft a fresh take on the classic. Instead of tequila as the base spirit, Abbott has opted for artisanal sake handcrafted on Granville Island.

GLASSWARE: Old-fashioned glass
GARNISH: Salt rim, dehydrated lime

- 1½ oz. (45 ml) Artisan SakeMaker Osake Junmai Nama Nigori
- 1 oz. (30 ml) Cointreau
- 1 oz. (30 ml) lime juice
- 10 drops (½ pipette) Ms. Better's Bitters Lime Leaf Bitters

1. Rim the old-fashioned glass with salt and fill the glass with ice.

2. Place all of the ingredients into a shaker cup and top with ½ cup (125 ml) of ice. Shake vigorously until the outside of the shaker frosts up to the top.

3. Strain the cocktail into the glass. Garnish with the dehydrated lime.

THE RICKSHAW

CUCHILLO, RAILTOWN

Bartender Coulter Noronha says his Rickshaw cocktail is a play on a Gin Rickey, using South Asian spices and Thai basil. "I called it the Rickshaw after the two- or three-wheeled passenger cart used in many Asian cities," he says.

"The yellow Chartreuse adds extra herbal and spice notes to the drink as well as being a digestif, making this drink the perfect follow-up to a big, spicy meal. It uses a local gin from Ampersand Distilling, which is very bright and citrus forward, further complementing the citrus notes of the drink."

GLASSWARE: Collins glass

GARNISH: Dehydrated lime wheel, Thai basil sprig

- 1½ oz. (45 ml) Ampersand Distilling Co Gin
- ½ oz. (15 ml) yellow Chartreuse
- ½ oz. (15 ml) simple syrup
- ½ oz. (15 ml) fresh lime juice
- 6 drops Bittered Sling Kensington Bitters (South Asian Spices with dry citrus)
- 4 to 6 Thai basil leaves
- 2 oz. (60 ml) soda water, to top

1. Put all of the ingredients, except the soda water, in a collins glass. Muddle the basil until it is fragrant.

2. Add crushed ice until the glass is almost full. Stir, mixing the basil into the ice.

3. Top with soda and garnish with the lime wheel and sprig of Thai basil.

BLACK HEART MANHATTAN

ODD SOCIETY SPIRITS, EAST VANCOUVER

This Black Heart Manhattan was created by Mia Glanz, bartender, emerging distiller, and daughter of Odd Society owner and head distiller Gordon Glanz (see also page 128). Odd Society's Salal Gin is a local take on sloe gin that uses salal berries foraged on the Sunshine Coast and Vancouver Island.

GLASSWARE: Coupe glass

GARNISH: 2 brandied cherries on a cocktail pick

- 1 oz. (30 ml) Odd Society Spirits Prospector Rye Whisky
- ½ oz. (15 ml) Odd Society Spirits Bittersweet Vermouth
- ½ oz. (15 ml) Odd Society Spirits Salal Gin
- ½ oz. (15 ml) black cherry juice (pure; not from concentrate)
- ½ teaspoon (5 ml) activated charcoal
- 1 dash Fernet-Branca
- Lemon peel

1. In a mixing glass, stir all of the ingredients, except the lemon peel, over ice.

2. Fine-strain the cocktail into the coupe.

3. Express the lemon peel over top; discard. Garnish with the two brandied cherries on a cocktail pick.

EMPRESS MARTINI

GLOWBAL, DOWNTOWN

The Empress Martini is the perfect combination of West Coast ingredients, starting with color-changing Empress 1908 Gin from Vancouver Island, rounded out with ingredients including chamomile tea and Crème de Cassis from Odd Society Distillery in East Vancouver. The crowning glory is local cedar tree aromatic hydrosol, which is used to create an edible smoke bubble.

GLASSWARE: Coupe glass
GARNISH: 8 drops Odd Society Crème de Cassis, cedar hydrosol, edible smoke bubble

- 2 oz. (60 ml) Empress 1908 Gin
- 1 oz. (30 ml) Chamomile Syrup (see recipe at right)
- 1 oz. (30 ml) egg white
- ¾ oz. (22.5 ml) lime juice

1. Add all of the ingredients to a shaker.

2. Shake without ice for at least 10 seconds. Add ice; hard-shake one more time.

3. Fine-strain the cocktail into the coupe. Garnish with 8 drops of crème de cassis.

4. Use an atomizer to spray cedar hydrosol over the drink; this coating will help to easily create an edible smoke bubble on the top using a Flavour Blaster.

CHAMOMILE SYRUP: Using a 1:1 ratio, prepare strong tea (steep it for 30 minutes), adding sugar and stirring until it dissolves.

A TASTE OF ASIA

WHITE RABBIT

SMOKING BARREL

EASTERN JEWEL

UMAMI MARTINI

RADIO GINZA

NĂM TỐT TEA

CÀ PHÊ MARTINI

SHISO MOJITO

Vancouver has always been city of immigrants, with newcomers from China, Japan, and Southeast Asia introducing flavors and ingredients into local cuisine and craft cocktails. At Old Bird, a modern Chinese bistro and bar, childhood nostalgia is channeled into a soothing yet boozy beverage by the recreation of flavors of the traditional White Rabbit candy. Japanese gins and sake are expertly blended at Grapes & Soda to bring out the best of each in imaginative ways, while Vietnamese coffee and pandan-infused vodka come together at Anh and Chi to create a supercharged interpretation of the Espresso Martini.

Whether shiso (perilla) leaves, yuzu juice, or tea (oolong, lapsang souchong, matcha, and ku ding), the ingredients that go into every cocktail are deliberate decisions. Each contributes a distinctive element (sweet, sour, bitter, smoky, earthy, aromatic, umami) that doesn't overpower the others.

Try to seek these ingredients out whenever possible to create a true representation of these inventive cocktails. Market stalls and apothecary-style shops and tea stores in Chinatown offer a wealth of Asian ingredients. And you can find items at everyday grocery stores and specialty supermarkets.

OLD BIRD

When Sophia Lin opened Old Bird in January 2020, her goal was to celebrate the stories of first- and second-generation immigrants, showcasing authentic Asian foods (from China, Thailand, Taiwan, and the Philippines) with a modern take. Located in Vancouver's Riley Park neighborhood, Old Bird—Miss Wong, a stern-looking lady—is the establishment's muse, "holding a cocktail in the left hand and a dumpling in the right."

Along with an array of cocktails (including zero-proof) enhanced with flavors such as five-spice powder, lychee, and ginseng, Old Bird offers "first try" and "cellar" tasting flights of *baijiu*, China's national spirit. Cellar includes a half ounce of Guo Jiao National Cellar 1573. Distilled from fermented sorghum, it's made by hand using traditional techniques by Luzhou Laojiao Company, the world's oldest continuously producing baijiu distillery, which dates back to 1573.

WHITE RABBIT

White Rabbit candy is a delicious childhood memory for kids who grew up in Asia," says Sophia Lin, owner of Old Bird, who hails from Shanghai. "This is a classic milk candy from China, light but creamy. We wanted to create a nostalgic drink with a little fun, hence this White Rabbit cocktail. The cocktail has a vanilla note, and it's bright and complex."

GLASSWARE: Collins glass

GARNISH: Dehydrated lemon coin, White Rabbit candy

- 2 oz. (60 ml) Black Tea (see recipe at right)
- 1½ oz. (45 ml) White Rabbit Vodka (see recipe at right)
- ½ oz. (15 ml) Lemon Oleo (see recipe at right)
- ⅓ oz. (10 ml) Lemon Hart Blackpool Spiced Rum
- ½ dash Ms. Better's Bitters Miraculous Foamer (optional)
- Orange blossom water spray, to top

1. Combine all of the ingredients, except the orange blossom water spray, in a cocktail shaker, and add ice.

2. Hard-shake for 40 seconds. Pour the cocktail into a collins glass with the ice.

3. Clip a dehydrated lemon coin and a piece of White Rabbit candy to the rim, then finish it off with a spray of orange blossom water.

BLACK TEA: Brew 4 bags of Lipton black tea in 4¼ cups (1 liter) of hot water. Cool and strain before use. Keep the tea refrigerated in an airtight container until ready to use.

WHITE RABBIT VODKA: Combine 25½ oz. (750 ml) of vodka, 3 oz. (90 ml) of condensed milk, ½ oz. (15 ml) of vanilla extract, and 1½ teaspoons (9 ml) of grated nutmeg. Mix thoroughly. Let the mixture sit for 24 hours and strain before use. Store in the refrigerator in an airtight container.

LEMON OLEO: Combine ½ cup (125 ml) of lemon zest with 1 cup (250 ml) of sugar. Let the mixture sit for at least 24 hours to extract the lemon oils. Pour in 1 cup (250 ml) of hot water and mix well. Let it cool and strain. Store in the refrigerator in an airtight container.

SMOKING BARREL

OLD BIRD, RILEY PARK

In this recipe, baijiu is married with two types of tea plus maraschino liqueur and lime to craft a modern cocktail with Chinese characteristics. "We are always seeking creative ways to make cocktails using the Chinese liquor baijiu that are delicious and will change people's minds about this hard liquor, as it is very important to Chinese culture," says Sophia Lin. The Smoking Barrel uses Bull 56 Baijiu infused with lapsang souchong tea that lends its signature smokiness and depth. "Sipping this cocktail reminds us of our Miss Wong's image—Miss Wong is Old Bird's inspiration—a bossy mafia lady wearing dark sunglasses and looking stern."

GLASSWARE: Coupe glass, chilled

GARNISH: Dehydrated, then burnt lime coin, fernet spray

- 1 oz. (30 ml) Lapsang Baijiu (see recipe below)
- 1 oz.(30 ml) lime juice
- 1 oz. (30 ml) Luxardo Maraschino Liqueur
- ⅓ oz. (10 ml) Green Tea Syrup (see recipe at right)
- 1 dash Ms. Better's Bitters Miraculous Foamer

1. Pour all of the ingredients into a cocktail shaker and add ice.

2. Shake hard for 40 seconds.

3. Double-strain into the chilled coupe. Garnish with the burnt lime coin and spray with fernet.

LAPSANG BAIJIU: Combine ¼ cup (60 ml) lapsang souchong tea with 2 cups (500 ml) of Bull 56 Baijiu. Let the mixture sit for at least 24 hours. Strain before use.

GREEN TEA SYRUP: Combine 10 bags of green tea with 1 cup (250 ml) hot water and 1 cup (250 ml) sugar. Mix thoroughly until the sugar is dissolved. Let it brew and cool down. Strain, then store in the refrigerator in an airtight container until ready to use.

EASTERN JEWEL

LAOWAI, CHINATOWN

Finding Laowai, a cocktail bar and dim sum parlor in Chinatown, takes a bit of tenacity. The speakeasy (read more on page 282) that opened in summer 2021 doesn't just test one's way-finding skills, it challenges palates with elegant cocktails that showcase complexity and style. That's fitting for the sophisticated space—whose name translates to "foreigner" in Mandarin—imagined by London firm Bergman Design House as a tribute to 1930s-era Shanghai. Walls wrapped in whorls of malachite are complemented by velvet-swathed seating, gilt birdcages, and glass fixtures. And the storybook cocktail menu is just as attention-grabbing, its recipes unquestionably original. In fact, in 2022, Laowai was crowned Best New Bar and placed fourth overall on the list of Canada's 50 Best Bars.

"All of our cocktails start out with historical research on individuals who actually existed in China, whether Chinese nationals or from other countries," says Alex Black, cocktail director and managing partner. He explains how he has found inspiration from figures such as Bodhidharma, who brought Buddhism to China. According to folklore, in an effort to stay awake during a nine-year meditation session, the sixth-century Indian priest tore off his eyelids. When they fell to earth, tea plants sprouted. Various types of tea are used in Laowai's recipes.

Black says such storytelling engages guests, and seeing selections of baijiu on the menu often excites second-generation Chinese-Canadian patrons familiar with the spirit, who sometimes bring their parents into the bar. With a background in distilling theory and bartender education (plus a raft of awards), Black initially crafted more approachable cocktails with baijiu to "scratch that itch of mine personally," he but was shocked when some people started asking for it neat. He started offering "stronger, funkier, weirder baijiu" and customers have been eager to learn about this spirit so integral to Chinese culture and community.

GLASSWARE: Nick & Nora glass

GARNISH: Orange rind

- 1½ oz. (45 ml) Chu Yeh Ching Chiew Light Aroma Baijiu
- ¾ oz. (22.5 ml) Tianjin Chile–Infused Yellow Chartreuse (see recipe below)
- ¾ oz. (22.5 ml) Ube Vermouth (see recipe at right)
- 3 drops Bittermens Burlesque Bitters

1. Pour all of the ingredients into a mixing glass.

2. Add ice. Stir and strain the cocktail into the Nick & Nora glass.

3. Twist the orange rind over top to release its oils then discard the rind.

TIANJIN CHILE–INFUSED YELLOW CHARTREUSE: Add 2¼ teaspoons (10 grams) dried Tianjin chile seeds (no pepper flesh) to a 25½ oz. (750 ml) bottle of yellow Chartreuse. Let the mixture sit for 24 hours. Strain before use.

UBE VERMOUTH: In a microwaveable container, mix together 750 ml off-dry Riesling, 200 grams sugar, 25 grams ube powder, 5 grams dehydrated salted plum, 3 grams bitter orange peel, 2 grams wormwood, 2 grams lapsang souchong tea, 1¼ grams salt, 1 gram gentian root, ½ gram angelica root, and ¼ gram ku ding (bitter green) tea. Microwave on high for 5 minutes. Stir the mixture well, ensuring all of the sugar is fully dissolved. Microwave again on high for 5 minutes. Double-filter through an oil filter and a coffee filter. Add 150 grams vodka (80 proof).

UMAMI MARTINI

GRAPES & SODA, SOUTH GRANVILLE

Satoshi Yonemori describes this cocktail as "my version of wet Martini with floral notes from shiso and umami from dashi." Yonemori is the award-winning bartender and co-owner of Grapes & Soda in South Granville (see 250). Originally from Japan, his expertise shines through in recipes like the Umami Martini. This drink blends and balances two types of sake and a trio of gins that impart essences and aromas of Japanese citrus (*yuzu*, *kabosu*, *amanatsu*, and *shequasar*), hints of *sansho* pepper, green tea, Japanese ginger, and cherry blossom.

GLASSWARE: Martini glass

GARNISH: Meyer lemon cheek or twist

- 1½ oz. (45 ml) Blended Japanese Gin (see recipe on page 205)
- 1½ oz. (45 ml) Blended Sake (see recipe on page 205)
- 4 dashes (2.5 ml) Meyer lemon juice
- 4 dashes (2.5 ml) Shiso & Dashi Tincture (see recipe on page 205)
- Shiso Salt (see recipe on page 205)
- Dashi Salt (see recipe on page 205)

1. Stir all of the ingredients together. Pour the cocktail into the martini glass.

2. Garnish with the Meyer lemon.

Satoshi Yonemori behind the bar

BLENDED JAPANESE GIN: Mix 2 parts Suntory Roku Gin, 1 part Nikka Coffey Gin, and 1 part Matsui Hakuto Fun Gin.

BLENDED SAKE: Mix 2 parts Kawatsuru Nama Genshu Sake with 1 part Momo Kawa Nigori Sake.

SHISO & DASHI TINCTURE: Combine 100 ml Shiso Tincture and 50 ml Dashi Tincture (see recipes below). Funnel into an eyedropper bottle.

SHISO TINCTURE: Combine 100 ml everclear and 10 grams shiso in a vacuum pack. Infuse in the freezer for a week. Use as needed.

DASHI TINCTURE: Combine 100 ml everclear, 3 grams of bonito flakes, and 1 gram of dried kombu in a vacuum pack. Infuse in the freezer for a week. Use as needed.

SHISO SALT: "It's more like salty shiso juice," says Yonemori. He uses a few drops per drink. Combine 15 ml kosher salt and 10 grams fresh shiso. Vacuum-pack the mixture tight and let it sit at room temperate for a few days. Squeeze the juice from the salt-and-shiso mix. Store the juice in an eye-dropper bottle in the refrigerator.

DASHI SALT: To make the dashi, combine 100 ml water and 10 grams bonito flakes. Let the mixture sit in the refrigerator overnight. The next day, bring it to a boil just for a second, then strain it right away. In a small frying pan, add 100 grams kosher salt and the bonito-dashi mixture. Simmer until all the moisture has evaporated. Cool. Vacuum-pack the salt and keep it refrigerated, using a small amount as needed. Yonemori uses "an earpick spoon of salt per drink."

RADIO GINZA

H TASTING LOUNGE, WESTIN BAYSHORE HOTEL, WEST END

H Tasting Lounge's newest cocktail menu is rooted in Asian influence and flavors. The Radio Ginza is a contemporary twist on a matcha latte, with subtle notes of banana and yuzu. Created by Taylor Kare, the idea for Radio Ginza was born from imagining what the upscale district of Ginza, Tokyo, was like in the late 1980s and early 1990s: a mix of city pop and anime music echoing through the streets while one is perched in a luxurious Tokyo café.

There's more at play here than imagination, too. The banana and yuzu give the matcha a bright green tone that evolves as the drink's temperature changes, akin to tuning to a radio station. (H Tasting Lounge is the sister restaurant to H2 Kitchen and Bar.)

GLASSWARE: Large tapered sake glass
GARNISH: Rice paper–printed anime face

- 2 oz. (60 ml) Matcha Soy Milk (see recipe at right)
- 1¼ oz.(40 ml) Plymouth Gin
- ⅓ oz. (10 ml) Tio Pepe sherry
- ¼ oz. (7.5 ml) Yuzu Syrup (see recipe at right)
- ¼ oz. (7.5 ml) Giffard Banane du Brasil

1. Add all of the ingredients to a shaker.

2. Shake for 10 to 15 seconds.

3. Double-strain the cocktail into the large sake glass.

4. Garnish with the rice paper anime print.

MATCHA SOY MILK: Mix 2½ tablespoons (20 grams) powdered matcha in 4¼ cups (1 liter) of soy milk.

YUZU SYRUP: Make 12 oz. (350 ml) syrup with 2 parts yuzu juice and 1 part white sugar. Boil together until the sugar is dissolved. Cool before use.

NĂM TỐT TEA

ANH AND CHI, RILEY PARK

Cuisine, cocktails, culture, and community. It's all part of an authentic experience at Anh and Chi, but at its heart, the Riley Park restaurant is formed around family. In the Vietnamese language, *anh* and *chi* translate to "older brother" and "older sister." Vincent Nguyen (chef and owner) and Amélie Nguyen (co-owner) are the siblings behind the laid-back yet refined operation, inheriting the work ethic of their parents Lý (executive chef) and Hoàng, who arrived in Canada in 1980 as refugees from Vietnam. They opened and ran the city's first pho specialty house, Pho Hoàng, in the same spot for thirty-three years.

Now the family has gained a new level of recognition, with Anh and Chi earning a Michelin Bib Gourmand in 2022. Although the recipes are rooted in Vietnam, modern touches are found in cocktails such as Năm Tốt Tea, which uses oolong tea, local elderflower liqueur, and gin infused with fresh blueberries.

GLASSWARE: Rocks glass

GARNISH: Rosemary sprig, three blueberries

- 1½ oz. (45 ml) Blueberry-Infused Bombay Sapphire Gin (see recipe at right)
- ½ oz. (15 ml) Odd Society Elderflower Liqueur
- ¾ oz. (22.5 ml) Oolong Tea Syrup (see recipe at right)
- ¾ oz. (22.5 ml) lemon juice

1. Combine all of the ingredients together in a shaker tin and fill with ice.

2. Shake hard for 15 seconds.

3. Double-strain the cocktail into the rocks glass and top with ice.

4. To garnish, slap the rosemary spring to bring out its oils and prop it up in the center of the ice. Drop the blueberries around it.

BLUEBERRY-INFUSED BOMBAY SAPPHIRE GIN: Infusing the blueberries into the gin intensifies the overall flavor of the gin without the drink becoming too sweet. In a mason jar, combine 25½ oz. (750 ml) London dry gin with 1 cup (340 grams) fresh blueberries. Sous vide for 4 hours at 160°F (71°Celsius). Let the jar cool before opening.

OOLONG TEA SYRUP: Steep ⅓ cup (25 grams) oolong tea in 3⅓ cups (800 ml) hot water for 6 minutes. Strain and squeeze the leaves and add 2 cups (400 grams) sugar. Stir to incorporate. Cool before using.

CÀ PHÊ MARTINI

ANH AND CHI, MOUNT PLEASANT

Pandan, when heated, gives off a delicious coconut aroma that works really well in this Espresso Martini riff," says bar manager Caleb Lopez. If you've been to Vietnam, you know creative caffeination extends to strong drip coffee paired with condensed milk, coconut, and even egg yolk. Lopez adds a splash of amaro in place of the coffee liqueur used in the original recipe.

❖

GLASSWARE: Teacup

GARNISH: Ground cocoa nibs

- 1¼ oz. (37.5 ml) Pandan-Infused Ampersand Per Se Vodka (see recipe below)
- 1 oz. (30 ml) Vietnamese coffee
- ¾ oz. (22.5 ml) Averna Amaro
- ½ oz. (15 ml) condensed milk
- 2 dashes Angostura bitters
- 2 dashes cocoa bitters

1. Combine all of the ingredients in a shaker tin. Fill with ice and shake hard for 15 seconds.

2. Double-strain the cocktail into the teacup.

3. Garnish by sprinkling the ground cocoa nibs in a line across one side.

PANDAN-INFUSED AMPERSAND PER SE VODKA: In a mason jar, combine 25½ oz. (750 ml) of vodka with 12 pandan leaves. Sous vide for 10 hours at 145°F (63°C). Let the mixture cool before opening.

SHISO MOJITO

East meets west at Miku, a sprawling light-filled space perched on the edge of Burrard Inlet overlooking the iconic five sails of Canada Place and the hulking shoulders of the North Shore mountains beyond. Although the Japanese restaurant is best known for its ultra-fresh seafood choices, especially *aburi* (flame-seared) sushi, its cocktails stand out as much as the cuisine.

The Shiso Mojito was created to be a light, refreshing drink that highlights the Japanese herb shiso (perilla), which comes from the mint family. Rather than the traditional rum, this take uses Tan Taka Tan as the base, the only Japanese shochu made from handpicked purple shiso leaves. Fresh shiso leaves and the spirit combine to offer a flavor profile of flowers and fresh-cut herbs, which balances the sweetness of the sugar and fresh-pressed lime juice.

GLASSWARE: Pilsner glass
GARNISH: Shiso leaf

- 1½ oz. (45 ml) Tan Taka Tan Shochu
- ⅓ oz. (10 ml) lime juice
- ⅓ oz. (10 ml) simple syrup
- 2 shiso leaves, torn

- 2 lime wedges
- Soda water, to top

1. Place all of the ingredients in a tin, except the soda water.

2. Add ice. Shake hard. Dirty-pour (don't strain) the cocktail into an ice-filled Pilsner glass.

3. Top with the soda water.

DRINKABLE FEASTS

DUNE

THERE & BACK

PUBLISHED MARTINI NO. 5

THE LIBERTY CAESAR

JUAN DE FUCA

AMATERASU

ARTEMIS

WAGYU & CHOCOLATE BOULEVARDIER

LEMON WET WORK

The kitchen and the cocktail have had a long relationship in Vancouver, largely because of the BC government's age-old histrionics over beer and spirits being consumed without sustenance. But the times they are a changing, and the upshot of such bureaucracy has been bartenders' culinary-minded approach to developing drinks.

Trevor Kallies, president of the Canadian Professional Bartenders Association (CPBA), takes me back to the 2000s, when such thinking was still the domain of fine dining. He recalls the nascent cocktail scene in Vancouver's bars when Freehouse Collective (then called Donnelly Group) opened the Granville Room. The gastropub was an elegant addition to the Granville strip, best known for its mashup of music venues and theaters such as the Commodore, the Orpheum, and the Vogue, huddled among the hostels, hotels, clubs, and pubs.

Kallies was one of its bartenders back then (he's now bar and beverage director for Freehouse Collective's dozen-plus establishments in Vancouver and Toronto). He says the Granville Room attracted a post-theater event crowd uninterested in the strip's high-volume bars hawking cheap drinks and alcohol-absorbing food on a street that has twice been ground zero for Stanley Cup riots. Instead, they wanted gastropub fare and were curious about classic cocktails.

At the Granville Room, "the chef did the legwork in terms of making simple syrup instead of sugar water in a bottle," says Kallies, and using freshly-squeezed lemons and limes, which wasn't exactly standard operating procedure for bars at the time. Small gestures made huge shifts in the industry as Vancouver's cocktail renaissance steadily picked up steam.

It's easy to imagine bartenders raiding the kitchen when coming up with cocktails that lean into flavors with an epicurean eye. At L'Abattoir, Dave Bulters infuses mezcal with mushrooms, while Published On Main's Dylan Riches brings bread, cucumber, and cheese to an aquavit cocktail. Meat plays a role both in the glass and as garnish at Bartholomew, where cacciatore salami–infused bourbon headlines a creation by Amine Zighem. Meanwhile, Max Curzon-Price and Andrew Kong at Suyo have elevated a humble and unsung hero—the parsnip—into a stunning sipper garnished with carrot dust and flakes of gold leaf. The idea of a drinkable feast as *amuse bouche* in Vancouver is infinitely appealing.

DUNE

SUYO, MOUNT PLEASANT

When Max Curzon-Price and Andrew Kong came up with the cocktail menu for SUYO, a modern Peruvian restaurant, they looked toward the South American nation's natural landscape—from the Andean mountains to its Amazon jungle, its coastal deserts to Pacific tides—and set off on a journey to create stories of symbiosis.

Curzon-Price is no stranger to such lofty aspirations. He was part of the team at Botanist Bar (see page 154) in the Fairmont Pacific Rim hotel, winning the 2019 Bols Around the World global bartending competition with Grant Sceney and Jeff Savage. (The trio bested 250 teams from more than forty countries.) In summer 2022, Curzon-Price brought his talents to the fifty-seat restaurant (with ten spots at the bar) while Kong came from H Tasting lounge (see page 206) in The Westin Bayshore Hotel.

One of those stories of ecological symbiosis that comes from the Coastal Deserts section of the menu is the Dune cocktail below. "It tells the tale of native arracacha parsnips—a hearty tuber that grows well along the coastal deserts of Peru," says Curzon-Price. "Dune is a testament to the way life finds a way to thrive underground when the heat of the day becomes too intense aboveground. The acidified parsnip replaces the need for lemon or lime juice, which can often steamroll delicate nuances, thus it allows the vegetal profiles to sit at the very forefront of the cocktail." Texture, of course, is also part of the equation, with parsnip juice lending a creaminess that's elevated by the egg white, culminating in "an incredible mouthfeel."

But Dune is only part of the symbiotic relationship; it connects to its sister cocktail Cacti. Dune's bee-pollen syrup and Cacti celebrate "the symbiotic nature between native Peruvian bees and the flowering succulents of the desert," says Curzon-Price. "Cacti is aged in beeswax so whilst the drinks have no shared ingredients, they do have similar profiles and intertwining stories."

GLASSWARE: Ceramic cup, frozen

GARNISH: Lavender bitters mist, carrot dust, gold flake

- 2 oz. (60 ml) Bombay Sapphire Gin
- 1 oz. (30 ml) Acidified Parsnip Juice (see recipe below)
- 1 oz. (30 ml) egg white
- 5 teaspoons (25 ml) Bee Pollen Syrup (see recipe below)
- 6 dashes Hay and Burdock Root Bitters (see recipe below)

1. In a shaker, combine all of the ingredients. First, emulsify the egg whites with a dry shake (shaken vigorously with a single ice cube to whip the egg whites) or with an immersion blender.

2. Fine-strain the cocktail into the frozen ceramic glass.

3. Mist with the lavender bitters, sprinkle with carrot dust, and carefully place the gold flake at the center of the carrot dust to represent the baking desert sun.

ACIDIFIED PARSNIP JUICE: Peel parsnips, cutting off the tip and tail of each vegetable. Soak them in water for a minimum of 6 hours. Cut the parsnips into 6-by-2-by-2-inch pieces. Juice them in a centrifugal juicer. Allow the parsnip juice to sit for a minimum of 1 hour, then carefully transfer it to another container. There should be a fine layer of parsnip "chalk" at the bottom of the original container—discard this.

Weigh* the parsnip juice and acidify it with citric, malic, and ascorbic acid, and salt. The ratios of acid to use by weight of the parsnip juice are as follows: citric acid, 3 percent; malic acid, 2 percent; ascorbic acid, 0.3 percent; and salt, 0.3 percent. (For example, 1,000 grams of parsnip juice would require 30 grams citric acid, 20 grams malic acid, 3 grams ascorbic acid, and 3 grams salt.) Stir well and ensure the acids have dissolved fully. Store the juice in a glass bottle and refrigerate.

BEE POLLEN SYRUP: Boil a pot of water, combining 35 grams of bee pollen for every 300 grams of boiling water. Remove the pot from heat. Allow it to sit for 25 minutes, stirring occasionally. Pass the pollen water through a coffee filter and allow it to drain fully. Weigh the remaining clear liquid and combine with an equal weight of granulated white sugar. Stir well to dissolve. Pour into a clean glass bottle and refrigerate.

HAY AND BURDOCK ROOT BITTERS: Combine 20 grams hay with 500 grams cachaça; allow the mixture to rest for a minimum of 4 weeks. Combine 30 grams dried burdock root with 500 grams vodka; allow it to rest for a minimum of 4 weeks. For best results, set the bitters somewhere with ample sunlight for an accelerated and more vibrant infusion.

Strain each product and weigh it. Combine 2 parts hay tincture with 3 parts burdock root tincture. Weigh the bitters and add 10 percent of the weight in simple syrup. For example: 200 grams hay tincture, plus 300 grams burdock root tincture, plus 50 grams of a 1:1 ratio of simple syrup.

THERE & BACK

PUBLISHED ON MAIN, RILEY PARK

Dylan Riches, bar manager at Published On Main, knows what it's like to be part of a winning team. When he worked at The Old Man in Hong Kong, the cocktail bar received two prestigious honors: the number one spot on Asia's Top 50 Best Bars list, and *Drink* magazine's Best Bar Team (Asia). The accolades keep coming. Riches was named global winner of the 2022 Hennessy My Way competition, while in the same year, Published On Main itself earned a Michelin star (wine director Jayton Paul was named Michelin Sommelier of the Year) on the heels of taking top place as Canada's Best New Restaurant, edging out ninety-nine others nationwide in the annual Canada's 100 Best lists.

Creativity knows no limits at this Riley Park restaurant where both cuisine and cocktails are provocative, playful, and executed with precision. Take the There & Back, for instance. Riches was inspired by its central ingredient, Linie Aquavit, which is filled into ex-sherry barrels and set off on ships, which circumnavigate the globe, to age. Contemplate that while sitting at the room's sleek bar and sipping.

"It is a practice the brand has done for more than 200 years," says Riches. "In Norway, where Linie hails from, aquavit is a common pairing for *brunost* ("brown cheese") cheese, which is made by slowly caramelizing whey, cream, and milk in a vat. The cucumber and rye bread syrup are a nod to a popular brunost, cucumber, and trout sandwich that is enjoyed for breakfast. Finally, in honor of the epic oceanic journey this incredible spirit undergoes, we use a touch of blue spirulina, which has a much softer and more neutral flavor compared to its green algae sibling."

GLASSWARE: Nick & Nora glass, chilled

GARNISH: Brunost cheese

- 1½ oz. (45 ml) Linie Aquavit
- 1 oz. (30 ml) Sour Cucumber Juice (see recipe at right)
- ¾ oz. (22.5 ml) Rye Bread Syrup (see recipe below)
- ½ oz. (15 ml) fino sherry
- ½ barspoon of blue spirulina
- ¼ oz. (7.5 ml) egg whites

1. Combine all of the ingredients in a shaker tin.

2. Dry-shake vigorously for 10 seconds, then add ice to the shaker and shake thoroughly.

3. Double-strain the cocktail into the chilled Nick & Nora glass.

4. To garnish, using a microplane, shred the brunost cheese on top of the cocktail—be generous with it.

RYE BREAD SYRUP: Toast ¾ cup (150 grams) rye bread, then slice it into small chunks. In a pot, combine the rye toast pieces with 2¼ cups (450 grams) white sugar and 2¼ cups (450 ml) filtered water. Simmer for 30 minutes, stirring regularly to integrate the sugar. Remove the pot from heat and strain through a fine-mesh sieve, making sure to press down on the bread to push out any syrup. It should yield approximately 2¾ cups (650 ml) of syrup.

SOUR CUCUMBER JUICE:
Chop 2 cups (500 grams) English cucumber into medium chunks. In a blender, combine the cucumber with 1 cup (250 ml) water; blend thoroughly. Fine-strain. Using a scale, measure the mass of the cucumber juice. Once you have the total mass of your juice, measure out 2 percent of that mass in citric acid, and 1 percent of the mass in tartaric acid. Combine both acids with the juice and blend again to integrate.

PUBLISHED MARTINI NO. 5

PUBLISHED ON MAIN, RILEY PARK

Smoke. Fire. Ice. Although this silky Martini doesn't leverage rye bread or cucumber, it embodies the essence of a drinkable feast with double doses of smokiness imparted from lapsang souchong tea and aromatic cedar smoke captured in a carafe. And, of course, there's that one well-placed frozen olive to feast on.

True to form, the Martini story at Published On Main is an ever-evolving anthology. Seven are on the books so far, each exploring hallmarks of the classic, then edging them far forward.

"This version has without a doubt been our most popular due to both its elegant presentation and deceivingly complex profile," says bar manager Dylan Riches, who created this cocktail with fellow bartender Dylan Zrobek. Inspired by the Burnt Martini, where the glass is rinsed with Scotch, Riches sought to explore the smoky aspect of the drink.

"Lapsang souchong, a black tea that's dried over a pinewood fire, carries a rich, smoky herbaceousness that is complemented by the brightness of the gunpowder tea–forward gin from Drumshanbo. Smoking the Martini with cedar wood brings not just a pleasing aroma but the texture of smoke, as it's mixed into the drink."

Lest you think that frozen olive for garnish is an afterthought, try again. It's more like an epilogue. "By the time the drinker has reached it, the olive has helped chill the Martini, and the Martini has helped thaw the olive," says Riches, adding, "Nothing worse than going to all the effort of chilling a drink, only to put something warm back into it."

GLASSWARE: Nick & Nora glass, chilled; carafe (for smoking)
GARNISH: Frozen olive

- 2½ oz. (75 ml) Drumshanbo Gunpowder Irish Gin
- ½ oz. (15 ml) Lapsang Souchong Vermouth (see recipe below)
- ½ barspoon Simple Syrup (see recipe below)
- 1 teaspoon (3 grams) cedar chips

1. In a mixing glass, combine all of the ingredients with ice. Stir for 30 seconds.

2. Strain the cocktail into a carafe. Using a glass-top smoker or smoking gun, smoke the cocktail in the carafe with 1 teaspoon (3 grams) cedar chips.

3. Cover the top of the carafe with a cork or plug and invert the carafe upside down to mix the cocktail with the smoke; hold the cork tight so you don't spill.

4. Place the frozen olive in the chilled Nick & Nora glass. Uncork the carafe and pour the Martini into the glass. Be dramatic about it.

LAPSANG SOUCHONG VERMOUTH: In a nonporous container, combine 9½ oz. (270 ml) Noilly Prat Dry Vermouth with 6½ oz. (180 ml) Dolin Blanc vermouth, and 1 teaspoon (4 grams) loose lapsang souchong tea, and let sit at room temperature for 45 minutes. Strain out the tea.

SIMPLE SYRUP: In a pot, combine 2 cups (450 grams) of white sugar with 2 cups (450 grams) of filtered water. Heat and stir until the sugar is fully dissolved. Keep refrigerated until ready to use.

THE LIBERTY CAESAR

THE LIBERTY DISTILLERY, GRANVILLE ISLAND

Full disclosure. I had to cajole, flatter, and basically beg Lisa Simpson, proprietor of The Liberty Distillery (see page 122), to give up the goods on this recipe. Of course, I'm overplaying her reluctance, and it wasn't because The Liberty's cocktail bar is hiding a top-secret recipe or hoarding Clamato juice. (In fact, *Vancouver* magazine ranked the distillery's Caesar the best in the city.) But in BC, the Caesar is expected. Sure, it's adored for brunchtime drinking and hangover fixing, but we almost take this umami bomb for granted because of its infinite reliability. The Liberty Caesar adheres to the tried-and-true recipe, with no over-the-top accoutrements to overshadow its purist form. If you want to level up from the original recipe, use Liberty's Endeavour Gin instead of the vodka.

GLASSWARE: Collins glass

GARNISH: Celery salt glass rim, spicy green bean and olive on a pick with a lime wedge, freshly grated horseradish, ground pepper

- 1 oz. (30 ml) The Liberty Distillery Truth Vodka
- ½ oz. (15 ml) lemon juice

- 3 drops Tabasco
- 5 drops Worcestershire
- Clamato juice, to top

1. Rim a collins glass with the celery salt.

2. Fill the glass with ice, vodka (or gin), lemon juice, Tabasco, and Worcestershire. Top with Clamato juice.

3. Garnish with a spicy green bean and olive on a pick with a lime wedge, freshly grated horseradish, and ground pepper.

CANADA'S OFFICIAL COCKTAIL: THE CAESER

Some people believe the Caesar (or Bloody Caesar) is merely a Canadianized version of the Bloody Mary. Sure. But the outlier ingredient is the "clam" in Clamato. Putting bivalves into a beverage seems like strange behavior to non-Canadians, and this beloved drink is often derided by our American cousins (they can also thank us for inventing Fireball Cinnamon Whisky back in the 1980s).

Yet most people are unaware that one of the ingredients in Worcestershire sauce that gives the Bloody Mary its depth is none other than that intensely fishy fish—the anchovy. So it's perfectly sane for Canadians to amplify the umami factor, giving some oomph to what would otherwise be a bloody boring Bloody Mary.

As most good Canadians know, a fellow named Walter Chell came up with the Caesar in 1969 when he was bar manager of The Owl's Nest in the Calgary Inn. Chell, an Italian immigrant, wanted to recreate the flavors of spaghetti *vongole* in a cocktail, to mark the restaurant's launch. According to one source, he spent months perfecting his recipe for what eventually became Canada's most celebrated cocktail.

In 2010, the Canadian Parliament proclaimed the Caesar as Canada's official cocktail, and in 2015, announced National Caesar Day would be celebrated on the Thursday before May ("two four") weekend, which is officially Victoria Day, named to honor the late queen's birthday. It normally falls around May 24, but a "two four" in Canadian parlance means a case of 24 beers.

JUAN DE FUCA

L'ABATTOIR, GASTOWN

The bar inside L'Abattoir restaurant has only nine seats, backed by windows overlooking the cobblestones of Maple Tree Square. Yet it snagged 49th place on Canada's 100 Best bars list in 2022, thanks to the creativity of the bartender team, which includes Dave Bulters. He describes this Juan de Fuca cocktail as "bitter, earthy, and slightly smoky; this drink was inspired by sips such as the Negroni and the Bijou."

GLASSWARE: Rocks glass
GARNISH: Hand-cut ice, freshly grated cinnamon

- 1 oz. (30 ml) Mushroom-Infused Mezcal (see recipe at right)
- ¾ oz. (22.5 ml) Esquimalt Bianco Vermouth
- ¾ oz. (22.5 ml) The Woods Amaro Chiaro
- 2 dashes Long Pepper Tincture (see recipe at right)

1. Combine all of the ingredients in a mixing glass over ice.

2. Stir briefly to dilute and chill. Then strain the cocktail into the rocks glass over hand-cut ice.

3. Grate a small amount of cinnamon over the exposed ice to garnish.

MUSHROOM-INFUSED MEZCAL: In an airtight vessel, combine a 25½ oz. (750 ml) bottle of mezcal with ½ cup (100 grams) fresh mushrooms. Slightly warm the infusion in a water bath for around 30 minutes. Allow the vessel to rest in a cool place for 3 to 4 days. Strain through a grease or coffee filter.

LONG PEPPER TINCTURE: In a mason jar, combine 1 cup (250 ml) high-proof vodka with 2¼ teaspoons (10 grams) long pepper. Allow the vodka to infuse for a week or more, agitating daily. Strain the tincture into a clean mason jar or airtight container.

AMATERASU

BARTHOLOMEW BAR, YALETOWN

Bartholomew Bar in Yaletown is an intimate space framed by warm woods and industrial elements offset by glimmers of glamor. Its ultra-long bar faces curved leather booths in prime position for guests to watch the shaking and stirring from their seats. Elevated classics can be had, like the barrel-aged Hanky Panky and the Pandan Daiquiri, while globe-trotting ingredients such as seaweed and edamame in the Amaterasu add another layer of invention that keeps things fresh for adventurous guests.

Bartholomew Bar's current house cocktail list is built around mythical entities and gods, with each drink representing the areas, flavors, and histories surrounding them, says Sean Raven, general manager. The Amaterasu, created by Dario Guaglione, for instance, gets its name from the Japanese celestial sun goddess. "So, we built a refreshing and vegetal Highball, highlighting some classic Asian flavors. Nori provides a hint of salinity into this drink and balances out the sweetness from the *umeshu*."

GLASSWARE: Collins glass
GARNISH: Lime twist, nori triangle, White Chocolate Paint
(see recipe next page)

- 1½ oz. (45 ml) Nori-Infused Tanqueray No. Ten Gin (see recipe next page)
- 1 oz. (30 ml) Edamame Puree (see recipe next page)
- 1 oz. (30 ml) lime juice
- ½ oz. (15 ml) umeshu
- Soda water, to top

1. Shake all ingredients, except the soda water, together for 10 seconds.

2. Strain the cocktail into a collins glass over ice. Top with soda water, giving a little stir at the end to mix.

3. Garnish with the lime twist, nori triangle, and White Chocolate Paint.

NORI-INFUSED TANQUERAY NO. TEN GIN: Mix a 25½ oz. (750 ml) bottle of Tanqueray No. Ten with 4 nori squares. Leave overnight to infuse. Strain before using.

EDAMAME PUREE: In a pan, cook 2¼ cups (500 grams) peeled edamame in 4¼ cups (1 liter) water for about 10 minutes, until the edamame is soft. Add 3¾ cups (750 grams) white sugar and let the sugar dissolve. Transfer the mixture to a Vitamix and blend.

WHITE CHOCOLATE PAINT: Melt white chocolate over a hot water bath. Once it's liquid, paint it on the glass. Refrigerate the glass until needed.

ARTEMIS

Like all bars worth their salt in Vancouver, serving sophisticated snacks or small plates can enhance the cocktail experience. Flavors play off one another, amplifying elements or creating contrasts. Bartholomew Bar offers an impressive selection of charcuterie and cheeses, plus what it calls accoutrements (pickles, spiced almonds) and enhancements (chicken butter and chutney) that present ample opportunities to experiment with cocktail pairings.

The Artemis, created by Amine Zighem, brings meatiness to the glass in three ways. First, continuing the theme general manager Sean Raven noted above, the cocktail's name comes from Greek mythology: Artemis is the goddess of the hunt and wild animals. And that influence extends into the drink's base spirit.

"When playing around with fat-washing for our new menu, it fit perfectly that we use a cacciatore salami, which is the classic Italian hunter's snack," says Raven. "Adding a salty, meaty, and slightly spicy depth to the drink, it's rounded off with a local Quadruple Sec, and fluffy egg white. Take a bite, take a sip. Repeat."

GLASSWARE: Coupe glass

GARNISH: Salami skewer

- 1½ oz. (45 ml) Cacciatore-Washed Buffalo Trace Bourbon (see recipe below)
- 1 oz. (30 ml) lemon juice
- 1 oz. (30 ml) egg white
- ½ oz. (15 ml) Sons of Vancouver Quadruple Sec
- ½ oz. (15 ml) Charcoal-Citrus Oleo (see recipe below)

1. Shake all of the ingredients without ice. Then shake with ice for 10 seconds.

2. Fine-strain the cocktail into the coupe.

3. Garnish with the salami skewer.

CACCIATORE-WASHED BUFFALO TRACE BOURBON: Chop 10⅗ oz. (300 grams) cacciatore salami into small slices. Place them in a vacuum bag along with 25½ oz. (750 ml) Buffalo Trace Bourbon. Seal the bag and sous vide for 2 hours at 140°F (60°C). Strain and use.

CHARCOAL-CITRUS OLEO: In a container, mix 2⅕ pounds (1 kilogram) juiced lemon husks and 2⅕ pounds (1 kilogram) white sugar. Leave the mixture overnight to macerate and extract essential oils. The next day, add 4¼ cups (1 liter) hot water to dissolve the sugar. Strain. Add about 2¼ teaspoons (10 grams) activated charcoal powder and mix.

WAGYU & CHOCOLATE BOULEVARDIER

MINAMI, YALETOWN

There's a delicate balancing act of flavors that have to come together to create something that's equal parts daring and delicious. One example at Minami (sister restaurant to Miku, page 212) is Stefan Lohka's inspiration for the Wagyu & Chocolate Boulevardier—an Espresso Negroni meets a Wagyu and Shiso Julep. Bourbon is washed with wagyu fat, then mixed with chocolate liqueur and, of course, sweet vermouth and Campari. While using Japanese A5 wagyu for fat-washing might seem decadent, it embodies the Japanese concept of *washoku*, delivering a truly elevated experience all in one glass. Lohka describes this cocktail as "a complex and ever-evolving journey through sweet, bitter, and umami, using a traditional and premium Japanese flavor to update a favorite classic."

GLASSWARE: Old-fashioned glass, chilled
GARNISH: Flamed orange zest, brandied cherry

- 1½ oz. (45 ml) Wagyu-Washed Maker's Mark Bourbon (see recipe at right)
- ½ oz. (15 ml) Chocolate Liqueur (see recipe at right)
- ½ oz. (15 ml) Poli Gran Bassano Red Vermouth
- ¼ oz. (7.5 ml) Campari

1. Add all of the ingredients to a mixing glass and stir over ice.

2. Strain the cocktail into the chilled old-fashioned glass.

3. Flame the orange zest over the glass, and garnish with the zest and a brandied cherry.

WAGYU-WASHED MAKER'S MARK BOURBON:
In a neutral container, add 6 oz. (170 grams) rendered
wagyu fat to 25½ oz. (750 ml) Maker's Mark Bourbon.
Place the mixture in the freezer overnight. Strain the
washed bourbon through a coffee filter.

CHOCOLATE LIQUEUR: Add 15 oz. (450
ml) cocoa nibs to 25½ oz. (750 ml) vodka; agitate. Let the mixture infuse for 8 days. Prepare
a vanilla simple syrup, boiling together 20 oz.
water, 30 oz. sugar, and 2 vanilla beans. Add
the vanilla simple syrup to the vodka and
cocoa nibs; agitate. Let it sit for 1 day. Strain
the liqueur through a coffee filter.

LEMON WET WORK

Fresh and seasonal cucumbers grown in BC are the foundation for Long Table Distillery's award-winning gin, which has earned recognition in the way of gold at the San Francisco World Spirits Competition in 2015 and bronze at the 2018 London Spirits Competition. This simple Lemon Wet Work recipe with lemon and basil lets the cucumber gin's citrus and pepper notes shine through.

GLASSWARE: Stemless wine glass
GARNISH: Cucumber, dried lemon, basil leaves

- 2 oz. (60 ml) Long Table Distillery Cucumber Gin
- ¾ oz. (45 ml) lemon juice
- ¾ oz. (45 ml) Lemon-Basil Syrup (see recipe below)
- Fever-Tree Sparkling Sicilian Lemonade, to top

1. Shake all of the ingredients, except the lemonade, together with ice.

2. Strain the cocktail into the wine glass over ice and top with Fever-Tree Sparkling Sicilian Lemonade (or another type of lemon tonic).

LEMON-BASIL SYRUP: In a pot over medium heat, place the rind of 1 full lemon, 6 basil leaves, 1½ cups (350 ml) sugar, and 1 cup (250 ml) water. Bring the mixture to a boil and let it simmer for 3 to 5 minutes. Cool before using.

FRUIT IN FOCUS

TÍO LOCO

POMONA

TROPPICINO

FIG TROUBLE IN LITTLE SUSU

INCAN REVIVAL

PINK SOUR

POPERIN PEAR

NIÑA PIÑA

NUBA EMPRESS

BEACH ROVER

Vancouver is a notoriously rainy city. We're obsessed with weather systems given cute names like "Tropical Punch" and "Pineapple Express" that bring balmy breezes off the ocean and create the type of torrential liquid sunshine that makes day drinking seem like a good way to wait out a storm (or an entire winter season).

When the clouds eventually lift in summer, cocktail menus are often influenced by seasonal fruit, like farm-fresh berries and juicy Shiro plums melted into a simple syrup. Yet you can't always wait for warm weather as the signal to sip something fruit-forward but balanced. In this city, it's like getting a much-needed mood-injection at any time of the year.

Even though each recipe in this chapter employs a healthy dose of fruit, sometimes the flavors are subtle support acts. Two honor classic fruit combos like pineapple and coconut: one offering a Peruvian treatment with Inca Kola, the other bringing the bitter with locally distilled amaro. Two others tame typically over-the-top passion fruit. And organic apple juice breaks free from the prosaic in two elegant cocktails that amplify the fruit in intriguing ways.

TÍO LOCO

GRAPES & SODA, SOUTH GRANVILLE

Satoshi Yonemori, award-winning bartender and co-owner of Grapes & Soda (and Farmer's Apprentice restaurant next door), is not afraid to experiment with outsize flavors and uncustomary ingredients. Thai chiles and homemade spruce syrup make an appearance in El Chapulín, his bold take on the Grasshopper cocktail (see page 90), while his Umami Martini (see page 202) uses a shiso-dashi tincture.

Yonemori has plenty to play with when innovating: the twenty-two-seat bar-bistro adjoins Farmer's Apprentice. Both embrace the ethos of using what's fresh, local, and in season. Excess ingredients from the restaurant elbow their way into Grapes & Soda's purees, syrups, and sodas.

The Tío Loco cocktail, as its name implies, is like an eccentric uncle—the life of the party who gets better the more booze you add. Flavors run the gamut from sweet to tart and spicy to funky. Yonemori uses a customized spiced rum and Howler Head Bourbon, which is bottled with natural banana flavor. Sea Buckthorn Liqueur, distilled in BC's Okanagan Valley, lends a touch of citrus with undertones of honey. But it's the house-made soda that takes this drink over the top.

It's an exceedingly complex cocktail to keep in check with the various recipes, yet Yonemori sums it up in few words: "Dark 'n Stormy on steroids." You may never go back to the original after sipping this stunner.

- 1 oz. (30 ml) lemon juice
- ⅘ oz. (25 ml) Jamaican rum
- ½ oz. (15 ml) House Spiced Rum (see recipe on page 253)
- ½ oz. (15 ml) House Tonic Syrup (see recipe on page 253)
- ½ oz. (15 ml) grapefruit juice
- ⅓ oz. (10 ml) Howler Head Bourbon
- ⅓ oz. (10 ml) Okanagan Spirits Sea Buckthorn Liqueur
- 2.5 ml pastis
- 2 oz. (60 ml) Salty Passion Fruit Ginger Curd Soda (see recipe below), to top

1. Shake all of the ingredients, except the soda, together with ice.

2. Dump the cocktail into the tiki mug and top with the soda. Give it a light stir. Add more ice if necessary.

3. Garnish with the bamboo straw, cocktail umbrella, and grapefruit wheels.

SALTY PASSION FRUIT GINGER CURD SODA: This recipe makes 1,000 ml. Combine 350 grams Passion Fruit Curd (see recipe below), 400 ml Ginger Juice (see recipe below), 100 ml Pineapple Tepache (see recipe below), 100 ml Vanilla Syrup (see recipe below), and 2.5 ml Maldon salt. Hand-blend them all together, then transfer the mixture to a soda siphon. Charge with two CO_2 cartridges.

PASSION FRUIT CURD: In a small pot, whisk together 250 grams organic cane sugar, 250 ml passion fruit puree, the zest of 8 lemons (finely chopped), 6 whole eggs, and 20 ml lemon juice. Heat the whole mixture over a hot water bath until the temperature hits 83°C (181°F). Pass the mixture through a fine chinois. Let it cool. Portion the curd into 350-gram vacuum-pack bags and freeze. Thaw as needed.

GINGER JUICE: Combine 400 ml filtered water with 80 grams organic ginger. Blend for 45 seconds; strain through fine chinois.

PINEAPPLE TEPACHE: Thoroughly combine 1 kilogram of pineapple pulp (the byproduct after juicing fresh pineapple), 1 kilogram organic cane sugar, and 1 liter filtered water. Vacuum-pack and let the mixture ferment for 3 to 4 days. Strain. Place the pineapple tepache in a pot, simmer for 5 minutes to pasteurise, then allow it to cool down. Vacuum-pack and freeze. Thaw as needed.

VANILLA SYRUP: Vacuum-pack 250 grams organic cane sugar, 250 ml filtered water, and half a vanilla bean pod (sliced open). Warm the pack in boiling water until the sugar dissolves. Cool the syrup down and strain it. Store it in the refrigerator for up to a week.

HOUSE SPICED RUM: In a 4-liter jar, combine 750 ml of each rum: El Dorado 12, Goslings Black Seal, Kingston Jamaican, and Havana Club 7 Year Old. Add 1 cinnamon stick, 1 piece of cassia bark, 3 star anise, 5 green cardamom pods, 3 whole cloves, 5 allspice, 2 vanilla beans (sliced open), zest of each: 1 grapefruit, 2 oranges, and 3 limes. Let the rum mixture sit for a week; strain before use.

HOUSE TONIC SYRUP: Simmer together the following ingredients for 15 to 20 minutes: 1,000 grams oleo saccharum (only zest and sugar; no juice), 1,000 ml filtered water, 2.5 ml salt, 30 ml citric acid, 2 dried five-flavor fruit (schisandra) berries (crushed), and 5 ml each: (dried) artichoke, wormwood, cinchona bark, orris root, gentian root, and 15 ml Caribbean sorrel (crushed). Strain the mixture through a fine chinois and allow it to cool. Vacuum-pack and freeze. Thaw as needed.

POMONA

The plump, round apple has been beguiling from its biblical beginnings. At NOX Restaurant, which borrows its name from the goddess of night in Roman mythology, the Pomona plays tribute to the goddess of fruit and orchards, placing the ancient apple at its center.

"For this cocktail, our main goal was to bring out the smokiness of the mezcal and the sweetness of the rum," says Sebastian Fuertes, bartender at NOX. "After a couple of tries, we thought it was missing a special something, so we decided to add milk into the creation, thus giving us an unexpected outcome." They discovered that the milk brought together those flavors, along with the earthiness of rosemary infused in a simple syrup.

"With this cocktail we intend to transport the customer to our Roman theme," says Fuertes, "giving the essence of elegance, smokiness, and herbal tones, resembling the goddess Pomona."

GLASSWARE: Nick & Nora glass

GARNISH: Citrus fruit, dried apple dust glass rim, 2 fresh rosemary leaves

- 1½ oz. (45 ml) organic apple juice
- ½ oz. (15 ml) mezcal
- ½ oz. (15 ml) dark rum
- ½ oz. (15 ml) Rosemary Syrup (see recipe on page 256)
- ¼ oz. (7.5 ml) homogenized milk (3.25 percent butter fat)

1. Rim a Nick & Nora glass with citrus fruit, then dip the glass in the dried apple dust. Chill the glass.

2. Place the organic apple juice, mezcal, dark rum, milk, and syrup in a shaker.

3. Add ice and shake vigorously to form a milky foam. Dump the ice into the glass and strain the shaken cocktail into it.

4. Garnish with the rosemary.

ROSEMARY SYRUP: In a pot, dilute 2⅕ pounds (1 kilogram) refined sugar with 4¼ cups (1 liter) water. Stir until the sugar disappears. Add 5 to 8 sprigs of fresh rosemary. Stir for 10 minutes over medium heat. Put the syrup in a container to cool to room temperature and store it in the refrigerator (yields 4¼ cups [1 liter]).

TROPPICINO

BAR SUSU, MOUNT PLEASANT

When The Whip Restaurant & Gallery shuttered in 2022 after operating for twenty-five years in a century-old brick building just off Main Street, Vancouverites lamented the loss of yet another institution. Then the brothers behind Twin Sails Brewing opened Bar Susu in the Edwardian-style edifice, ushering in a new era of natural wines, craft cocktails, and inventive dishes (Bar Susu is the sister restaurant to Published On Main, page 223). The imbibing experience alone is worth trying to find a seat at the back bar, to sip a rotating menu of drinks such as Fig Trouble at Little Susu and Troppicino, the latter of which has an unexpected blend of ingredients.

"We're really leaning on the tropical notes of lighter-roast coffee beans and loading this cocktail with Guatemalan Ron Zacapa 23, some fluffy pineapple juice, and passion fruit flavor. These characteristics are bolstered with—of course—some amaro (Bar Susu style) and coffee liqueur," says Joe Casson. The bar director at Susu explains the cocktail's name is a portmanteau of "tropical" and "cappuccino," "where tropical escapism and Espresso Martinis meet."

"Passion fruit is a bit of a playground bully in cocktails but plays very nicely with other bullish flavors such as coffee and amaro. It really lifts each component of the drink—the coffee, the rum, not to mention the silky pineapple element. This is a lighter and fruitier expression of Espresso Martini as opposed to the more bitter coffee-forward style."

GLASSWARE: Coupe glass, chilled

GARNISH: Edible flower

- 1 oz. (30 ml) Cold Brew Concentrate (see recipe below)
- ⅔ oz. (20 ml) Ron Zacapa No. 23
- ⅔ oz. (20 ml) Cynar
- ⅔ oz. (20 ml) Kahlúa
- ⅔ oz. (20 ml) pineapple juice
- ¼ oz. (7.5 ml) Giffard Passionfruit Syrup
- 2 dashes Angostura bitters

1. Add all of the ingredients to a metal mixing tin or cocktail shaker.

2. Add a large tablespoon of crushed ice and use a hand blender to blitz it all together and fluff it up.

3. Fine-strain the cocktail into the chilled coupe. Garnish with an edible flower.

COLD BREW CONCENTRATE: Use a Vitamix to blend 5 cups (400 grams) whole coffee beans (light to medium roast; "I like beans from House of Funk," says Casson) in batches, not too fine but not too coarse, either—we want flavor and extraction. Add the grounds to a plastic container, along with 5¼ cups (1,200 grams) water. Stir well and let the coffee sit for 12 to 18 hours for best results. Strain through a coffee filter to finish. Bottle the concentrate and store it for up to 3 days. This recipe is a 3:1 ratio and yields about 4¼ cups (1 liter).

FIG TROUBLE IN LITTLE SUSU

BAR SUSU, MOUNT PLEASANT

GLASSWARE: Rocks glass

GARNISH: Fig leaf rondelle, orange coin

- 1 oz. (30 ml) Fig Leaf-Infused Aalborg Taffel Aqvavit (see recipe below)
- 1 oz. (30 ml) Cocchi Dopo Teatro Vermouth Amaro
- ¾ oz. (22.5 ml) Noilly Prat Ambre Vermouth
- ¼ oz. (7.5 ml) Shiro Plum Syrup (see recipe below)

1. Add all of the ingredients (3 oz. [90 ml] if batching) to a mixing glass and stir over ice. Then strain the cocktail into a rocks glass over a big ice cube.

2. Garnish with the fig leaf rondelle, and express the orange coin over the drink.

SHIRO PLUM SYRUP: Heat 1 cup (250 grams) of whole Shiro plums in 3 cups (700 grams) water and bring to a rolling boil. Turn down the heat to a simmer. Cook for 30 minutes and let the plums break down. Add 3½ cups (700 grams) sugar and dissolve. Let cool and store in the fridge for up to 2 weeks. Yields approximately 4¼ cups (1 liter).

FIG LEAF-INFUSED AALBORG TAFFEL AQVAVIT: Rinse 1¼ cups (200 grams) fresh fig leaves with water; pat dry. To sous vide, add leaves to a vacuum-sealable bag, along with a 25½ oz. (750 ml) bottle of Aalborg Taffel Aqvavit. Seal and cook at 131°F (55°C) for 3 hours. Let the mixture cool, strain, and rebottle.

INCAN REVIVAL

ANCORA, DOWNTOWN AND WEST VANCOUVER

When Ancora opened the first of its two waterfront locations in 2015, it introduced the city to Nikkei cuisine (Peruvian-meets-Japanese), complemented by a wine list and creative cocktails.

Katie Slacks and Sephora Jade Janz teamed up to craft this Peruvian take on a classic—the Corpse Reviver No. 2—using South America's favorite soda, Inca Kola.

The Incan Revival highlights Peruvian pisco, herbaceous Chartreuse, and the distinctive flavors of Inca Kola (lemon verbena and cream soda), while imparting a subtle hint of anise from locally made Ms. Better's Pineapple Star Anise Bitters.

GLASSWARE: Nick & Nora glass, chilled
GARNISH: Rum cherry

- 1½ oz. (45 ml) Barsol Pisco
- ¹⁷⁄₂₀ oz. (25 ml) Toasted Coconut and Pineapple–Infused Inca Kola Syrup (see recipe at right)
- ¹⁷⁄₂₀ oz. (25 ml) lime juice

- ½ oz. (15 ml) Cointreau
- ⅕ oz. (7 ml) yellow Chartreuse
- 2 dashes Ms. Better's Pineapple Star Anise Bitters
- Pastis mist, to top

1. Combine all of the ingredients except the pastis in a shaker. Add ice and shake.

2. Double-strain into the chilled Nick & Nora glass.

3. Mist with the pastis and garnish with the rum cherry.

TOAST COCONUT AND PINEAPPLE–INFUSED INCA KOLA SYRUP: Combine 5 cans Inca Kola with 1 cup (250 ml) raw, toasted coconut, 1 cup (250 ml) sugar, and one fresh pineapple, cored and chopped. Simmer for 35 minutes or until the mixture has thickened. Let the syrup cool completely before using.

PINK SOUR

UVA Wine & Cocktail Bar is a compact space that shape-shifts from Italian café by day to sexy cocktail den by night. Its Aperitivo Hour has long lured locals to the edge of Yaletown, and its riffs on classic sour ratios keep things interesting. A case in point is the Pink Sour, crafted by bartender George Brand-MacFarlane. His interpretation of the sour formula, using lower-alcohol (23 percent ABV) Amaro Montenegro, pairs its bitter and herbal elements (plus notes of orange and chocolate) with the subtleness of vodka. Lemon juice lends the sour, balanced out by the tart and sweet of cranberry cocktail and cocktail syrup.

GLASSWARE: Rocks glass

GARNISH: 4 Infused Strawberries (see recipe at right)

- 1½ oz. (45 ml) Amaro Montenegro
- 1 oz. (30 ml) egg white
- ¾ oz. (22.5 ml) lemon juice
- ½ oz. (15 ml) vodka
- ½ oz. (15 ml) cranberry cocktail
- ½ oz. (15 ml) cranberry syrup

1. Add all of the ingredients to a shaker and dry-shake. Then add ice and shake again.

2. Strain the cocktail into the rocks glass over ice.

3. Garnish with the infused strawberries.

INFUSED STRAWBERRIES: In a portion cup, place dehydrated strawberries with equal parts Amaro Montenegro, vodka, and crème de cacao to cover. Let the strawberries sit overnight or until they are soft and chewy but not soggy.

A SOUR FAMILY

Even though they don't have the word in their names, the Daiquiri, Margarita, and Sidecar all fall into the family of cocktails called *sours*. Each includes a base spirit, some citrus, and a sweetener.

Daiquiri: white rum, lime juice, simple syrup

Whiskey Sour: whiskey, lemon juice, simple syrup

Margarita: tequila, lime juice, orange liqueur

Sidecar: brandy, lemon juice, orange liqueur

One of the common ratios for sours is 2:1:1 (2 parts spirits, 1 part sour, 1 part sweet), but bartenders will change up the proportions of sour and sweet to suit their preference—and you should, too. Don't be afraid to play with the types of citrus and sweetener, either. The Hemingway Daiquiri, for example, sticks with 2 oz. (60 ml) white rum, but boosts the sour, using ¾ oz. (22.5 ml) of lime juice and ½ oz. (15 ml) of grapefruit juice, and trades simple syrup for ½ oz. (15 ml) of maraschino liqueur. (*Technically* . . . when liqueur is used as a sweetener, instead of simple syrup, the cocktail falls into the daisy family.)

The Amaretto Sour in action (see page 112)

POPERIN PEAR

At first glance, the Poperin Pear appears icy and the ingredients intimidating, like murderous Lady MacBeth. But there's plenty playful about this cocktail, especially its Shakespearean name, which actually comes from a line spoken by Mercutio to Romeo in *Romeo and Juliet*. The meaning of the alliterative phrase whose first use harks back to 1594 ("O, that she were an open-arse, or thou a popp'rin pear!") can be filed firmly in two categories—pearl-clutching or smirk inducing—as I was illuminated by *Green's Dictionary of Slang*. Don't say I didn't warn you. Go on. Look it up.

GLASSWARE: Coupe glass, chilled

- 1 oz. (30 ml) unfiltered apple juice
- ¾ oz. (22.5 ml) Bombay Sapphire gin
- ¾ oz. (22.5 ml) Grey Goose La Poire Vodka
- ¾ oz. (22.5 ml) yellow Chartreuse
- ½ oz. (15 ml) lemon juice
- ¼ oz. (7.5 ml) honey

1. Shake all of the ingredients together with ice.

2. Strain the cocktail into the chilled coupe.

NIÑA PIÑA

Never underestimate the power of drinking a cocktail under a *palapa* on Alimentaria Mexicana's patio (seemingly afloat in the middle of Granville Island, which isn't actually an island) to transport you to far-flung climes.

Crafted by award-winning bartender Sabrine Dhaliwal (see page 307), the Niña Piña is a globe-trotting concoction of Peruvian pisco, pineapple, and Spain's stalwart Licor 43, which has an ingredient list that remains under embargo, aside from five of the 43: lemon, orange, vanilla, coriander, and tea.

GLASSWARE: Old-fashioned glass
GARNISH: Pineapple wedge

- 1½ oz. (45 ml) pisco
- 1½ oz. (45 ml) pineapple juice
- ⅔ oz. (20 ml) lemon juice
- ½ oz. (15 ml) Licor 43
- ⅓ oz. (10 ml) Vanilla Syrup (see recipe below)

1. Shake all of the ingredients together.

2. Serve with ice in an old-fashioned glass.

3. To garnish, place the pineapple wedge on the rim of the glass.

VANILLA SYRUP: Make a 1:1 simple syrup. Add one vanilla bean, split open lengthwise, scraping the seeds into the syrup. Let it sit for several hours. Store it in the refrigerator.

NUBA EMPRESS

NUBA (VARIOUS NEIGHBORHOODS)

Nuba is a place that gets carnivores excited about cauliflower (seriously), and puts local ingredients in its Lebanese dishes and drinks, including its Turmeric Ale (a collab with Faculty Brewing Co.) and the chameleonic Nuba Empress, one its most popular sips. Think of it as an upscale Gin and Juice using Empress 1908 Gin. The spirit gets its regal indigo hue from butterfly pea blossom, and when citrus and agave are invited to the party, the cocktail transforms into a lovely shade of lavender.

GLASSWARE: Rocks glass
GARNISH: Orange slice, sprig of dried lavender

- 2 oz. (60 ml) Empress 1908 Gin
- ½ oz. (15 ml) orange juice
- ½ oz. (15 ml) lemon juice
- ¼ oz. (7.5 ml) agave juice

1. Add all of the ingredients to a mixing glass and stir to combine.

2. Pour the cocktail into the rocks glass over ice.

3. Garnish with the orange slice and sprig of dried lavender.

BEACH ROVER

ODD SOCIETY, EAST VANCOUVER

Not only is this cocktail a delicious lesson on how to change up tropical ingredients to add more dimension to a drink, it's also a quick course in what qualifies as whiskey in Canada (see below).

Reminiscent of the classic Piña Colada, this cocktail combines coconut, pineapple, orange juice, and a splash of amaro to lend some bitter to the sweet. But instead of traveling to warmer climates for rum like a Piña Colada would, the Beach Rover served in Odd Society's cocktail lounge doesn't stray far from home. It uses Odd Society Mongrel Unaged Spirit, which is made from 100 percent BC-grown rye and distilled on-site.

Whether you call it "white dog," "white lightning," or the more sophisticated "white whiskey," Mongrel Unaged Spirit, as its name infers, goes right into the bottle after distillation. No wood. No aging. It can't *legally* be called whiskey or rye, though at 50 percent ABV, this dog sure has bite.

GLASSWARE: Coupe glass

GARNISH: Freshly grated nutmeg, coconut shavings

- 2 oz. (60 ml) pineapple juice
- 1¼ oz. (37.5 ml) Odd Society Mongrel Unaged Spirit
- 1 oz. (30 ml) Coconut Cream (see recipe at right)
- 1 oz. (30 ml) fresh-squeezed orange juice
- ¾ oz. (22.5 ml) Odd Society Mia Amata Amaro

1. In a metal tin, shake all of the ingredients together with ice (wet shake).

2. Shake without ice until frothy (dry shake).

3. Strain the cocktail into the coupe.

4. Garnish with freshly grated nutmeg and coconut shavings.

COCONUT CREAM: In a mason jar, combine 1 can coconut milk and an equal volume granulated sugar. Shake to dissolve the sugar; no heat is required.

CANADIAN WHISKY 101

What qualifies as "whisky" (like the Scottish, we spell it without the "e") in Canada? By law, to be called Canadian whisky, Canadian rye whisky, or simply rye whisky, it must stick to certain requirements with respect to the alcoholic distillates (made from cereal grain[s] mashed and distilled in Canada), aging (a minimum of three years, in small wood—a barrel not exceeding 700 liters), and minimum alcohol by volume (40 percent). Unlike, say, bourbon, there aren't any rules about the type of wood or whether casks have to be new wood or not.

Curiously enough, to be called "rye" in Canada, there's no minimum percentage of grain required (the United States requires the "mash bill" to be a minimum of 51 percent rye grain). It just has to exhibit some of the characteristics that rye grain would provide.

IF FOUND, PLEASE RETURN TO

TRADE   S OF SV   MARK

SONS OF VANCOUVER DISTILLERY LTD. NORTH VANCOUVER. BC

Barrel No

172

SPEAKEASIES AND

TO FRIGHTEN A MONGOOSE

FRENCH TICKLER

BEHIND BLUE EYES

BOURBON SFORZANDO

THE RED AND NARROW

SMOKE SHOW

LE CACI

"Be cool. Speak easy."

There's no need to whisper when you're inside today's modern speakeasies. Yet there's still something subversive about having to crack a code or piece together clues to find a hidden entry (often in plain sight), even though Prohibition is long in the past.

An aura of exclusivity exists at today's speakeasies, and the price of entry is often only ingenuity and a sense of play. You get to walk through the wardrobe, peek behind the wizard's curtain, and journey through to Wonderland—if you're game. Of course, I won't share speakeasy spoilers (why ruin the fun?), but if you read carefully, you'll find clues in the copy.

Below are recipes from bona fide speakeasies plus a couple of (somewhat) hidden local haunts that are oases smack in the city. Passwords aren't required at those watering holes, but the payoff is a bang-up view of Vancouver to enjoy while sipping a craft cocktail.

TO FRIGHTEN A MONGOOSE

BAGHEERA, CHINATOWN

We hide. You seek." It's the cryptic message (and rules of engagement) on Bagheera's Instagram feed, along with carefully dropped hints on how to find Chinatown's newest speakeasy, which opened in January 2023. The game is afoot, and you'd best be on the lookout for a Chinese betting house with a façade as fake as AstroTurf.

Created by the team behind Laowai (see page 199), Bagheera is named for the black panther in *The Jungle Book*. Rudyard Kipling writes, "A black shadow dropped down into the circle. It was Bagheera the Black Panther, inky black all over, but with the panther markings showing up in certain lights like the pattern of watered silk."

That evocative image and nostalgia are beautifully embodied in the tunnel-like space that's as glamorous inside as the streets outside are gritty. The luxe look, which includes a train car with sixty seats offering a "passage to India," comes courtesy of London's Bergman Design House. It's a gorgeous drinking den where literature inspired the libations created by Alex Black, cocktail director and managing partner.

More than 1,000 antique coins and bracelets line the walls behind a forty-two-foot bar, a prominent display of tiger-blue onyx and hand-carved reclaimed teak. Settle in here or repair to the drawing room to seek out the so-called "cabinet of curiosities" filled with whiskeys that are somewhat hard to find—like a certain speakeasy in Chinatown.

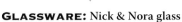

GLASSWARE: Nick & Nora glass

GARNISH: Grated nutmeg

- 1½ oz. (45 ml) Beefeater Gin
- 1 oz. (30 ml) pistachio orgeat

- 1 dash Scrappy's Cardamom Bitters
- 2 dashes Bittermens Herbal Honey Bitters

1. Pour all of the ingredients into a mixing glass.

2. Add ice. Stir and strain the cocktail into the Nick & Nora glass.

3. Garnish with the grated nutmeg.

FRENCH TICKLER

KEY PARTY, MOUNT PLEASANT

Key Party is a sexy speakeasy fronted by a slim anteroom masquerading as an accountancy office. You can imagine a bespectacled number cruncher working away using props such as a rotary-dial phone and Rolodex. It's a buttoned-up foil for what lies inside the lounge, where things swing in a decidedly different direction. Evoking the 1960s and 1970s, Key Party (owned by the same folks as The Narrow Lounge, see page 86) presents modern and classic cocktails with tongue-in-cheek names such as Bee on Your Knees (see page 76) and French Tickler, a take on the French 75. Other offerings include The Shades of Grey, an obvious reference to the erotic book and series (set in Seattle but filmed in Vancouver, as usual), and the Pearl Necklace garnished with a toasted marshmallow.

Don't let any of that distract you from the stylish space, which is ultra-dark as you enter. As your eyes adjust, a world opens up with ruby-red walls and a mural spread across the wall behind the bar. And if you pull back the velvet curtain in the cozy environs to head to the loo, oddly enough, you'll might find yourself hankering for a taste of BBQ. Debaucheries aside, Key Party expects people to keep it classy, its rules stating: "Everyone is welcome to the party. No racist, sexist, homophobic or hateful attitudes or talk will be tolerated."

GLASSWARE: Coupe glass, chilled
GARNISH: Edible orchid

- 2 oz. (60 ml) pineapple juice
- 1½ oz. (45 ml) vodka
- ½ oz. (15 ml) Chambord
- Jacob's Creek Sparkling Shiraz, to top

1. Add everything, except the sparkling wine, to a shaker.

2. Shake with ice until the pineapple juice froths.

3. Double-strain the cocktail into the chilled coupe.

4. Add the sparkling wine to top.

5. Garnish with an edible orchid or other flower you may find pretty.

BEHIND BLUE EYES

LAOWAI, CHINATOWN

Even though number 8 is the go-to for good fortune in Chinese culture, dumpling-loving denizens know to roll the dice on lucky number 7 to find Laowai. The Chinatown hotspot is both cocktail bar and dim sum parlor, and it's all about curating an experience, from the opulent décor to the award-winning drinks. Both embody elements of Asia. In the 1930s, Shanghai was a decadent city and the gilded interiors of Laowai transport guests to that golden era, complemented by modern baijiu-based drinks, among other creations from Alex Black, cocktail director and managing partner. The menu isn't just about what's on offer, it's an educational peek at the lives of people who either lived or passed through China long ago. Those influences underpin the choice of ingredients in each drink.

GLASSWARE: Rocks glass

GARNISH: Dehydrated pear

- 2 oz. (60 ml) Lapsang Souchong–Infused Bourbon (see recipe on page 289)

- 1 ¾ tablespoons (25 ml) Asian Pear Syrup (see recipe on page 289)

- 4 drops Apothecary Bitters Mystic Caravan Smokey Pear Bitters

- Absinthe (for rinsing the glass)

1. Pour all of the ingredients into a mixing glass.

2. Add ice. Stir and strain the cocktail into an absinthe-rinsed rocks glass.

3. Garnish with the dehydrated pear.

LAPSANG SOUCHONG—INFUSED BOURBON: In a clean container, mix together 3½ teaspoons (15 grams) lapsang souchong tea to 25½ oz. (750 ml) Evan Williams Botted-in-Bond Bourbon. Let the mixture sit, sealed, at room temperature for 24 hours. Strain off the tea leaves, return the liquid back to the bottle, and seal.

ASIAN PEAR SYRUP: In a heavy-bottomed pot, combine 1½ cups (350 grams) fresh Asian pear juice, 1¼ cups (300 grams) organic cane sugar, 1 teaspoon (5 grams) gomme powder, ¼ cup (45 grams) water, and 3½ teaspoons (15 grams) Maldon salt. Bring the mixture to a light boil for 1 minute, stirring frequently. Pour it into a clean container, leaving it to cool to room temperature. Once it's at room temperature, place it in a glass container and refrigerate.

BOURBON SFORZANDO

THE SANDBAR, GRANVILLE ISLAND

You'd be forgiven for thinking The Sandbar on Granville Island is playing hide-and-seek. First, you need to get to this waterfront hub, ideally on foot or by ferry, then make your way by a wooden boardwalk to a building tucked underneath the Granville Street Bridge's steel struts. Then it's up two flights of stairs, through the main restaurant and bar, passing a wooden boat suspended from the ceiling, and through a glass door to get to the heated rooftop terrace (open year-round) with a warming fireplace and views of False Creek shimmering in the shadow of Yaletown's vertiginous glass towers.

The cocktail menu offers a super selection, like the Bourbon Sforzando. "Smoky, sweet, and bitter elements blend beautifully in this modern variation of a classic Manhattan," says The Sandbar's Dawid Karczmarczk. As the story goes, bartender Eryn Reece crafted this cocktail during her time at Death & Co. in New York City. Its name is a musical term that refers to playing with a particular accent or stress. The Bourbon Sforzando is definitely an up-tempo take on the original with herbal nuances from the Benedictine.

GLASSWARE: Highball glass

GARNISH: 2 cherries

- 1 oz. (30 ml) Maker's Mark Bourbon
- 1 oz. (30 ml) mezcal
- ½ oz. (15 ml) Benedictine
- ½ oz. (15 ml) sweet vermouth
- 3 dashes Angostura bitters

1. Add ice and all of the ingredients to a mixing glass.
2. Stir generously.
3. Strain the cocktail into the highball glass over a large ice cube.
4. Garnish with the cherries.

THE RED AND NARROW

THE NARROW LOUNGE, MOUNT PLEASANT

Not every mystery is meant to be revealed. Often, it's more fun to unravel the secret on your own. The Narrow is one of those places you'll never really stumble upon, especially given the randomness of its location at the end of Mount Pleasant, on the edge of Olympic Village, fully within East Van, yet not exactly off the beaten path.

Yet plenty of locals know to look for the single red light that lets you know the bar is open for business. After all, The Narrow snuck into the 44th spot on Canada's 100 Best bars list in 2022. The outside looks a little sketchy (deep disguise), but a few steps lead you down into this ravishing rabbit hole with shoulder-to-shoulder bar seats and a handful of high-top tables and booths. There's a vintage vibe with a touch of taxidermy, and chandeliers capping off the décor. It's deliciously dark. But in this warren awaits another surprise: a covered outdoor patio with picnic tables that's open during summer.

GLASSWARE: Double rocks glass, chilled
GARNISH: Salt (for the glass rim), maraschino cherry on a skewer

- 2 oz. (60 ml) blanco tequila
- 1 oz. (30 ml) lemon juice
- ½ oz. (15 ml) Crème de Cassis de Dijon by L'Héritier-Guyot
- ½ oz. (15 ml) egg white

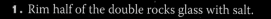

1. Rim half of the double rocks glass with salt.

2. Shake all of the ingredients with ice.

3. Strain the cocktail into the glass over fresh ice.

4. Garnish with a skewered maraschino cherry.

SMOKE SHOW

BAYSIDE LOUNGE, WEST END

The Bayside Lounge has the trifecta: a laundry list of cocktails, a retro vibe (the bar has been in operation for more than four decades), and heady views of English Bay from its almost hidden spot above Denman Street in Vancouver's West End. The long room is dominated by a sunken circular bar that seems to radiate good vibes in an unfussy atmosphere with vintage appeal. If you'd darkened the doorway of the Bayside years back, you would have found rotary phones at each table, encouraging guests to ring each other and chat, low-tech Tinder style. Day drinking is especially appealing if you can snag a seat near the window and look out at the ocean while sipping a Sazerac, the Smoke Show, Le Caci (both below), or one of the forty-plus drinks on the menu.

GLASSWARE: Rocks glass

GARNISH: Burnt orange peel

- 2 oz. (60 ml) ruby red grapefruit juice
- 1 oz. (30 ml) Montelobos Mezcal
- 1 oz. (30 ml) Grand Marnier
- 1 oz. (30 ml) lime juice
- ¾ oz. (22.5 ml) simple syrup (1:1)
- Splash of egg whites
- 4 dashes orange bitters

1. Thoroughly shake all of the ingredients with ice and strain the cocktail into the rocks glass.

2. Garnish with the burnt orange peel.

LE CACI

BAYSIDE LOUNGE, WEST END

GLASSWARE: Old-fashioned glass
GARNISH: 2 blackberries on a stir stick, lemon twist

- 1 oz. (30 ml) Ungava Gin
- ½ oz. (15 ml) Dubonnet
- ½ oz. (15 ml) Pimm's No. 1 Cup
- ½ oz. (15 ml) orgeat
- ½ oz. (15 ml) green Chartreuse
- 2 lemon wedges (squeezed)
- 3 blackberries (muddled)
- Fentimans Ginger Beer, to top

1. Shake all of the ingredients together with ice, except the ginger beer and Chartreuse. Strain the cocktail into an old-fashioned glass.

2. Add the green Chartreuse to an empty glass and light it on fire.

3. Immediately double-strain the Chartreuse into the old-fashioned glass. Slowly add ice.

4. Top with ginger beer and stir. Garnish with the blackberries and lemon twist.

CONTEMPORARY
COCKTAILS

PLUTO

CORNER STORE

GREYSCALE

SUN ALSO RISES

QUETZALCACAO

MUMBAI NIGHTS

NIGHT MOVES

GOTHAM GIRL

LULUMELON

212

HIDEAWAY HONEY

LATE NIGHT WALKER

SANTIAGO

At its most basic, a cocktail is an accumulation of ingredients. But it's also an accumulation of ideas. Breaking down components into broad categories. Playing with proportions and flavor pairings to find the sweet spot on a Venn diagram where everything intersects. Understanding the nuances of every element that goes into the end product, from glass to garnish. Techniques are tested. Prototypes are deconstructed, redefined, rebuilt.

Creating a cocktail is often about engineering an experience that suffuses the senses from the moment the drink greets the guest—aroma, texture, and taste. Everything choice is considered, right down to the decision of what to *omit*. Skipping the straw lets the cocktail's aroma announce its presence before the first sip. Opting for a wheel of lime as garnish instead of a wedge means the guest is less likely to squeeze those extra drops of citrus into the cocktail, disrupting its fine balance.

Many of the cocktails in this chapter, like Sabrine Dhaliwal's Greyscale, are object lessons in ingenuity and iteration. Others are evocative of people and places, like Havana's Santiago and 1181's Lulumelon—a proudly pink drink that owner Todd Hoye says is "a nod to Davie Village's most sexy and chic clientele." Meanwhile, Nick Appleby at AnnaLena is shooting for the stars with Pluto and its massive moon. Each recipe is transportive in its own way.

PLUTO

ANNALENA, KITSILANO

Creating a contemporary cocktail takes time and commitment. Guests need to give up a bit of both if they want to savor one of the concoctions crafted by Nick Appleby, head bartender at Anna Lena. Appleby takes us into orbit with his explanation of his otherworldly cocktail. "Pluto's largest moon is Charon. It's so massive relative to the dwarf planet that they orbit each other. Umeshu is a beast, and so is amaretto. They 'orbit' each other in flavor profile; however umeshu is more pronounced so amaretto is the Charon here."

GLASSWARE: Crystal-cut collins glass
GARNISH: Kodama Ice Co ice spear

- 1 oz. (30 ml) Yamaguchi Tomari Umeshu
- ½ oz. (15 ml) Sons of Vancouver No. 82 Amaretto
- ¼ oz. (7.5 ml) Pierre Ferrand Dry Curaçao
- Cava, to top
- Lemon twist

1. Pour the amaretto and umeshu into the collins glass. Lower the ice spear into the drink.

2. Top with cava and gently stir to incorporate everything evenly.

3. Express the lemon twist over top of cocktail; discard the twist.

CORNER STORE

Appleby brings us back down to earth with his Corner Store, whose name refers to the fact that some of its ingredients (sugar, koji, cacao nibs) can be found in your typical, well, corner store or market. (He admits the name is also a nod to the sneaker and streetwear shop on Main Street.) Intense and complex, the cocktail is meant to be sipped slowly. "The umami from the koji and herbaceousness of Fernet-Branca contrast the long finish imparted by the cacao-soaked bourbon and rich coffee liqueur," says Appleby. "The use of añejo tequila bridges these flavor profiles and balances the drink."

GLASSWARE: Rocks glass

GARNISH: Orange twist

- 1 oz. (30 ml) Cacao-Soaked Old Forester Bourbon (see recipe below)
- ½ oz. (15 ml) Koji Syrup (see recipe below)
- ⅓ oz. (10 ml) Sheringham Distillery Coffee Liqueur
- ⅓ oz. (10 ml) Gran Centenario Añejo Tequila
- 1 teaspoon (5 ml) Fernet-Branca

1. Add all of the ingredients to a mixing glass and stir for 30 to 45 seconds.

2. Pour the cocktail into the rocks glass over a king ice cube.

3. Garnish with the orange twist.

CACAO-SOAKED OLD FORESTER BOURBON: Mix about 3 tablespoons (25 grams) cacao nibs with 25½ oz. (750 ml) Old Forester Bourbon. Let the cacao nibs soak for 24 hours before straining them out and either discarding or repurposing them.

KOJI SYRUP: This recipe makes 2 cups (500 ml). In a pot over medium heat, add 1 cup (250 ml) water and 1 cup (250 grams) white sugar; stir to dissolve. Remove the pot from heat and add 2 oz. (60 ml) of *shio koji*. Often used as a marinade for cooking, shio koji is composed of fermented grain (*koji*), salt (*shio*), and water. It's possible to find it in grocery stores. Using shio koji allows for easier distribution within the syrup. The koji will settle over time (nothing to worry about), so it will need to be gently agitated before using it in a cocktail.

GREYSCALE

THE CHICKADEE ROOM, CHINATOWN

It might seem strange for a cocktail bar to be wedged inside a restaurant in Chinatown that's feted for fried chicken and ribs that come with Vietnamese *nuoc cham*. Yet ever since The Chickadee Room opened inside Juke Fried Chicken in June 2020, its free-spirited appeal has drawn crowds for cocktails shaken and stirred by bar manager Sabrine Dhaliwal. In 2015, Dhaliwal won Belvedere Vodka's international competition ("The Challenge") to create a twist on a Martini. She is currently a national brand ambassador for Moët Hennessy spirits.

The Chickadee Room pays tribute to the 1980s, so Dhaliwal says she wanted to create a cool take on a classic cocktail but with a hit of the decade's vibe, which ushered in neon colors, Lean Cuisine, and the start of molecular gastronomy. (Not to mention the bar's lineup of cocktails inspired by 1980s songs "Electric Avenue," "Livin' On a Prayer," and "Don't Stop Believing.")

"This cocktail is taking it back a bit to a classic Gin Sour from the 1800s with a small amount of 'molecular gastronomy' to change the syrup—and voilà—the Greyscale was born."

Although Dhaliwal makes it sound easy, she notes this cocktail went through many iterations before becoming list-worthy. "The syrup was worked over and over again with different cooking methods and different forms of black limes to see which would give the most balanced and crowd-pleasing flavor profile."

GLASSWARE: Nick & Nora glass, chilled
GARNISH: Black Lime and Black Sesame Powder (see recipe below)

- 2 oz. (60 ml) London Dry Gin
- ⅔ oz. (20 ml) lime juice
- ½ oz. (15 ml) Black Lime and Sesame Syrup (see recipe below)
- 1 egg white

1. In a shaker tin, crack a fresh egg, adding the white and discarding the yolk.
2. Add the gin, lime juice, and Black Lime and Sesame Syrup.
3. Shake without ice.
4. Add ice; shake vigorously for 7 to 10 seconds.
5. Fine-strain the cocktail into the chilled Nick & Nora glass.
6. Garnish with the Black Lime and Black Sesame Powder.

BLACK LIME AND SESAME SYRUP: In a medium saucepan, add 3 to 5 crushed black limes and 2 cups (500 ml) water. Allow the mixture to simmer and reduce the volume by half. Add 2 cups (500 grams) white sugar; without boiling, stir until all of the sugar is dissolved. Add the syrup to a blender. Add 2 tablespoons (30 ml) black sesame paste. Blitz the lime husks and dissolve any remaining sugar. Pass the syrup through a cheesecloth to remove any solids. Store the syrup in an airtight container in the refrigerator. The syrup will keep for 4 weeks.

BLACK LIME AND BLACK SESAME POWDER: Grind 3 black limes into a fine powder. Pass the black lime powder through a fine sieve. Pass 3 tablespoons (45 ml) black sesame powder through a fine sieve. Combine both powders and store the result in an airtight container.

SUN ALSO RISES

There are few people or places in the city that have racked up as many accolades as the bar team at the Fairmont Pacific Rim. Grant Sceney, creative beverage director, presides over the hotel's cocktail program, which encompasses the glamorous Lobby Lounge and RawBar on the hotel's main level and Botanist Bar upstairs (see page 154). Originally from Australia, Sceney's talents led him to be named 2014 World Class Canada Bartender of the Year. And in the Michelin Guide's first foray into Vancouver in 2022, Sceney and head bartender Jeff Savage of Botanist won the inaugural *Michelin Guide* Vancouver's Exceptional Cocktails award.

The team often hosts visiting bartenders such as Masahiro Urushido, bartender and owner of Katana Kitchen in New York City, and the crew from Singapore's much-lauded bar Manhattan, where they come together to design a signature-cocktail menu.

Thirsty travelers and locals alike can find a sofa or lounge chair framed by fireplaces and floor-to-ceiling glass, or grab a seat at the bar to order classic cocktails and longtime faves such as the fruity and floral Geisha cocktail or the Sun Also Rises, which marries tequila and tamarind.

- Tajín seasoning (for the glass rim)
- 1½ oz. (45 ml) Don Julio Reposado
- 1 oz. (30 ml) Tamarind Syrup (see recipe below)
- ½ oz. (15 ml) Ron Zacapa Rum
- ½ oz. (15 ml) grapefruit juice
- ½ oz. (15 ml) lime juice

1. Rim one side of the rocks glass with Tajin seasoning. Fill the glass with ice.

2. Combine all of the ingredients in a shaker with ice. Shake thoroughly.

3. Strain the cocktail into the rocks glass.

4. Garnish with the dehydrated grapefruit wheel.

TAMARIND SYRUP: In a pot, place 2¼ cups (500 grams) tamarind paste and 9 cups (2 liters) water. Note: Use the thick and hard tamarind paste, not cooking tamarind or cooking concentrate. Bring to a boil. Let the mixture boil for 5 minutes and remove it from heat. Take a muddler or rolling pin and use it to carefully break up the tamarind. Don't let the hot water splash on you.

Break up the tamarind as much as you can, then pour the water and tamarind through a sieve into a new pot. Use the back of the spoon to break up and push the tamarind through the sieve as much as possible. Repeat this step twice. Then put the mixture back on heat. Add 10 cups (2 kilograms) sugar and stir until it is dissolved. Remove the pot from heat. Once the syrup has cooled, store it in a container in the refrigerator.

BARTENDER TIP: Put the tamarind syrup into a squeeze bottle when ready to use for making drinks.

QUETZALCACAO

CUCHILLO, RAILTOWN

Coulter Noronha shares how his Quetzalcacao cocktail is named after the diety Quetzalcoatl ("feathered serpent"). According to folklore, he says, the Aztec god brought the cacao plant down from the sacred mountains to the Aztec people who made the first hot chocolate, called *xocolatl*, which translates to "bitter water," and was mixed with cacao and spice. "This cocktail pays tribute to the original chocolate drink by combining spice with rich dark chocolate bitterness, accented by the complex notes of the *destilado de pulque*. Xocolatl was used for many ceremonies by the Aztecs and the Quetzalcacao is a great drink to have on a night of celebration."

GLASSWARE: Coupe glass, chilled

- 1½ oz. (45 ml) Estancia Destilado de Pulque
- 1 oz. (30 ml) Ancho Cacao Syrup (see recipe at right)
- ½ oz. (15 ml) Ancho-Infused Dark Rum (see recipe at right)
- 6 drops Apothecary Bitters The Darkness Cacao Coffee Bitters

1. Combine all of the ingredients in a mixing vessel.

2. Add ice and stir.

3. Strain the cocktail into the chilled coupe.

ANCHO CACAO SYRUP: Bring 1 cup (250 ml) water to a boil and add 1 cup (250 ml) sugar. When the sugar is dissolved, add 1 tablespoon (15 ml) vanilla extract, 2 tablespoons (30 ml) ancho chile powder, and ¼ cup (60 ml) cocoa powder. Stir the mixture and remove it from heat after 1 minute. Fine-strain the syrup to remove any large particles.

ANCHO-INFUSED DARK RUM: In a container, place 25½ oz. (750 ml) dark rum of your choice and 1 dried ancho chile pepper. Let it sit for a minimum of 24 hours. Fine-strain the rum and put it back in its bottle.

MUMBAI NIGHTS

VIJ'S, CAMBIE

It didn't take a 2022 Michelin Bib Gourmand award to put Vij's on the map. Or Mark Bittman writing in the *New York Times* that Vij's is "easily among the finest Indian restaurants in the world." Vancouverites have known this since this beloved go-to opened in 1994, waiting in lines curving around the block for their turn to experience the hospitality and modern Indian cuisine created by husband and wife team Vikram Vij and Meeru Dhalwala.

Of course, the cocktail program has been developed to echo the food, says bar manager Marc Smolinski. It features classic cocktails with an Indian twist. The Mumbai Nights, he says, "is a riff on the Cosmopolitan, infused with Indian glitz and glamor prevalent in Bollywood." He infuses Belvedere Vodka with black cardamom seeds and rose petals, which lend spicy and aromatic floral notes to the spirit. "It's vibrant and dynamic," says Smolinski, "like the nightlife in India's most cosmopolitan city."

GLASSWARE: Coupe glass, chilled
GARNISH: Edible silver glitter or silver foil

- 1 oz. (30 ml) Rose and Black Cardamom–Infused Belvedere Vodka (see recipe at right)
- 1 oz. (30 ml) pomegranate juice
- ½ oz. (15 ml) Lillet
- ½ oz. (15 ml) simple syrup
- ½ oz. (15 ml) lime juice
- ¼ oz. (7.5 ml) Luxardo Maraschino Liqueur
- ¼ oz. (7.5 ml) pomegranate molasses

1. Add all of the ingredients to a mixing tin. Add ice and shake.

2. Double-strain the cocktail into the chilled coupe.

3. Garnish with the edible silver glitter or a small piece of edible silver foil.

ROSE AND BLACK CARDAMOM–INFUSED BELVEDERE VODKA: Crush 1 teaspoon (5 ml) black cardamom pods; remove the seeds inside. Add the seeds and ⅓ cup (75 ml) dried rose petals to a sealable glass or plastic container. Pour in 25½ oz. (750 ml) Belvedere Vodka. Seal the container and let the infusion macerate for 48 hours. Fine-strain the infused vodka into a clean sealable glass or plastic container.

NIGHT MOVES

HAWKSWORTH COCKTAIL BAR, ROSEWOOD HOTEL GEORGIA, DOWNTOWN

Every cocktail has a story, one etched in mind over the ages or languishing in obscurity. Night Moves, created in 2013 by Hawksworth's former head bartender, Cooper Tardivel, gets its name from the title track of the eponymous 1976 album by Bob Seger & the Silver Bullet Band. The tune and lyrics are deeply nostalgic for some. Time marches forward, but both song and cocktail recipe are worth a foray into the past.

White port and rum might seem like an odd pairing until you uncover the complexity of Ron Zacapa No. 23. The rum is aged using a solera system, a typical method for blending ports and sherries across vintages. Ron Zacapa No. 23 is a blend of six- to twenty-three-year-old rums aged in ex-American whiskey and Pedro Ximénez sherry casks, creating complex aromas and flavors like vanilla, oak, and dried fruit. Averna balances the booze-forward beverage with a hit of bittersweet.

GLASSWARE: Coupe glass, chilled
GARNISH: Maraschino cherry

- 1½ oz. (45 ml) Ron Zacapa No. 23
- ¾ oz. (22.5 ml) Taylor Fladgate White Port
- ½ oz. (15 ml) Amaro Averna
- 4 dashes Angostura bitters

1. Stir all of the ingredients over ice.
2. Strain the cocktail into the chilled coupe.
3. Garnish with the maraschino cherry.

GOTHAM GIRL

GOTHAM STEAKHOUSE & BAR, DOWNTOWN

In a city whose skyline is strikingly young, the 1933 art deco stunner of a building (designed by architect Max Downing) occupied by Gotham Steakhouse & Bar stands out. The expert bar team has crafted a similarly standout signature cocktail called Gotham Girl. A fresh libation, it's balanced by a slight spicy note from the cardamom bitters and the sweetness of hibiscus floral syrup and given an extra twinkle from sparkling wine. Its rosy, bubbly appearance, topped with a pretty brandied cherry, feels flirtatious and fun, from first sight to first sip. Local musicians and DJs contribute to the lively atmosphere in the lounge, an ideal spot for pre-dinner cocktails or a nightcap.

GLASSWARE: Champagne flute

GARNISH: Brandied cherry on a spear

- 1 oz. (30 ml) Bombay Sapphire Gin
- ¾ oz. (22.5 ml) lemon juice
- ¾ oz. (22.5 ml) Giffard Hibiscus Syrup
- 1 dash Scrappy's Cardamom Bitters
- 4 oz. (120 ml) Mumm Napa Brut Prestige sparkling wine, to top

1. Combine all of the ingredients, except the wine, into an ice-filled Boston shaker.

2. Shake hard to a count of 5.

3. Strain the cocktail into the champagne flute.

4. Top with the sparkling wine.

5. Garnish with a speared brandied cherry resting on the rim of the flute.

LULUMELON

1181 LOUNGE, DAVIE VILLAGE

DJs, dance floor, drag shows, drinks—all in Davie Village. It's non-stop action at 1181 Lounge, an award-winning club and lounge in the heart of the West End's LGBTQIA2S+ community. It's easy to walk right past 1181's understated exterior where rainbow crosswalks, purple banners, pink benches, and rows of restaurants are all vying for attention. Yet owner Todd Hoye has put together an enticing lineup of cocktails, from classics such as Margaritas and Moscow Mules to the playfully named bourbon-based In the Buff, and the Pink Brazilian, a mix of Cachaça, muddled grapefruit juice, and more.

But one beverage outshines all the others. "The Lulumelon has been 1181's most popular signature cocktail for nearly a decade," says Hoye. "Its sweet, fresh ingredients make it a delicious, easy-drinking choice, especially in the summer months. Its vibrant pink color and its eye-catching garnish are a nod to Davie Village's most sexy and chic clientele," he says, adding "1181's most famous cocktail gets its unique name from a clever play on the name of Vancouver's most famous homegrown athletic brand, Lululemon."

GLASSWARE: Stemless martini glass
GARNISH: Watermelon wedge

- 2 to 3 cubes fresh-cut watermelon
- 2 oz. (60 ml) Absolut Vodka
- 1 oz. (30 ml) Monin Passionfruit Syrup
- 1 oz. (30 ml) cranberry juice
- ½ oz. (15 ml) lime juice

1. Place the watermelon cubes into a cocktail shaker. Muddle until the watermelon becomes a puree.

2. Add ice, plus all the other ingredients. Shake vigorously.

3. Using a cocktail strainer and fine-mesh sieve, double-strain the drink into the stemless martini or cocktail glass. Ensure that no watermelon chunks, pulp, or seeds make it into the final product.

4. Garnish with the watermelon wedge.

212

CAFÉ MEDINA, DOWNTOWN

Stepping inside Café Media downtown is an ideal way to be transported from the West Coast to the Mediterranean. Hearty brunch dishes such as fricassee and cassoulets are complemented by a roster of beverages that channel far-flung locales, such as the Five Miles to Tangier (a take on the Espresso Martini); the Casablanca Sour, imparted with Earl Grey tea; and the aptly named 212 (Morocco's country code). This cocktail is as vibrant green as the wild mint of Zenata. This refreshing summer sipper gets an herbaceous lift from the cult classic French liqueur green Chartreuse, the herbal digestif known for its piercing green hue and mysterious recipe of 130 herbs and spices, known only by the two monks who make the blend.

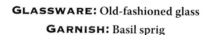

GLASSWARE: Old-fashioned glass
GARNISH: Basil sprig

- 4 basil leaves
- ½ oz. (15 ml) lemon juice
- 1½ oz. (30 ml) gin
- ½ oz. (15 ml) green Chartreuse
- ½ oz. (15 ml) St-Germain Elderflower Liqueur

1. Muddle the basil leaves with the lemon juice in a cocktail shaker.

2. Add the rest of the ingredients with ice and shake until cold.

3. Double-strain the cocktail into an old-fashioned glass over ice.

4. Garnish with the basil sprig.

HIDEAWAY HONEY

CAPO & THE SPRITZ, YALETOWN

Chamomile tea and amaro might seems like an odd couple, but the perfect pairing that inspired Alannah Taylor, bar manager of Capo & the Spritz, was her grandparents. She recalls drinking tea with her grandmother while her grandfather got into the amaro. "Smooth, delectable, and light, this offers complexity without being overpowering," says Taylor. "The slight dill and caraway undertones of the aquavit add a spice that complements the chamomile—all poured over a locally crafted polarized ice cube."

GLASSWARE: Rocks glass
GARNISH: Gypsophila (baby's breath) bunch

- 1 oz. (30 ml) Chamomile-Infused Bornholmer Akvavit (see recipe on page 326)
- ½ oz. (15 ml) Quintessentia Amaro Nonino
- ½ oz. (15 ml) fresh-squeezed lemon juice
- ½ oz. (15 ml) Honey Simple Syrup (see recipe on page 326)
- Kodama Ice Co polarized ice cube

1. Combine all of the ingredients, except the ice cube, in a Yarai mixing glass.

2. Add ice (not the cube) and stir for 20 seconds.

3. Strain the cocktail into a rocks glass over the Kodama polarized ice cube.

4. Garnish with the gypsophila bunch.

CHAMOMILE-INFUSED BORNHOLMER AKVAVIT: Place 25½ oz. (750 ml) of Bornholmer Akvavit and 4 chamomile tea bags into a container. Let the ingredients infuse for 24 hours then strain.

HONEY SIMPLE SYRUP: Add 4¼ cups (1,000 ml) of honey to 6 cups (1,500 ml) of boiling water. Stir to dissolve the honey and let the syrup cool.

LATE NIGHT WALKER

CAPO & THE SPRITZ, YALETOWN

In Alannah Taylor's twist on the classic Negroni, she says "Johnnie Walker Black offers a punch while Lillet Blanc and Disaronno calm it down. Having coffee without the coffee is such an added treat and goes such a long way to make a late-night walk even better."

GLASSWARE: Rocks glass
GARNISH: 3 espresso beans

- 1 oz. (30 ml) Johnnie Walker Black
- 1 oz. (15 ml) Lillet Blanc
- 1 oz. (15 ml) Disaronno Amaretto
- 2 dashes Bittered Sling Arabica Coffee Bitters
- Kodama Ice Co polarized ice cube

1. Combine all of the ingredients in a Yarai mixing glass.
2. Add ice; stir for 20 seconds.
3. Strain the cocktail into the rocks glass over the Kodama polarized ice cube.
4. Garnish with the espresso beans.

SANTIAGO

HAVANA, COMMERCIAL DRIVE

Agave spirits are in constant contention with rum as the top choice for cocktails at the community gathering place and gallery on Commercial Drive known as Havana. "With its regionally specific and unique flavors, mezcal is incredible to use in cocktails, as it tends to vary in flavor by nature of its production," says Alexa Greenman, beverage director. "Creating mezcal is a labor of love, and we try to bring that attention to detail and quality into our industry by giving each drink that same level of dedication."

A staff favorite, the Santiago was named after one of Oaxaca's agave-growing regions. "We utilized the spiced, fruity backbone of Sombra, combined with its rich smoky notes, to create complementary flavors. Each component should accentuate the mezcal's inherent qualities, bringing together the story of mezcal and creating a drink where each sip gives you something different and therefore wanting to come back for more."

GLASSWARE: Etched old-fashioned glass
GARNISH: Dehydrated pear slice

- 1½ oz. (45 ml) Sombra Mezcal
- 1½ oz. (45 ml) Poached Pear and Ginger Syrup (see recipe at right)
- 1 oz. (30 ml) lemon juice
- ½ oz. (15 ml) Lillet Blanc
- ¼ oz. (7.5 ml) orgeat

1. Add all of the ingredients to a shaker tin; shake vigorously.

2. Double-strain the cocktail into the etched old-fashioned glass over ice.

3. Garnish with the dehydrated pear slice.

POACHED PEAR AND GINGER SYRUP: In a large container, combine 4¼ cups (1 liter) of hot water and 4¼ cups (1 liter) of granulated sugar. Stir to dissolve. Roughly chop 8 pears, 2 lemons, and 2 large pieces of ginger (peeled and sliced). Add these to the simple syrup. Transfer the mixture to a pot. Bring the mixture to a boil and leave it on low; simmer to poach for at least 25 minutes. Once finished, transfer the mixture back to the container to let sit in liquid for at least 2 hours. After steeping, strain out the solids from the syrup.

(MOSTLY) SOBER SIPS

LAVANDA FIZZ

JAMAIQUITA LEMONADE

COMMERCIAL DRIVE

MARGUERITE DAISY

THE VITALIZER

WATERMELON CUCUMBER SODA

FAIRMONT WATERFRONT'S BEES KNEES

I s there a time for temperance? Absolutely. People abstain from alcohol for an array of reasons. Some like to start a new year with Dry January, which seems like a new trend, but any establishment lamenting empty bar seats thanks to post-holiday indulgence can blame the Finnish Government. It kicked off the first campaign in 1942, as part of the war effort (alcohol was needed for ammo) but it only lasted a year.

It wasn't until 2014 that a UK charity called Alcohol Change established the modern version of annual alcohol abstinence, which migrated west under cringey portmanteaus such as Soberuary or Drynuary. So here's a mini PSA: In January 2023, the Canadian Centre on Substance Use and Addiction replaced its 2011 *Low-Risk Alcohol Drinking Guidelines*, now stating that having between three and six standard drinks per week puts people at moderate risk; seven or more is "an increasing high risk." The upshot? Less is better.

Whatever the reason for mindful drinking—such as winding down the evening with a zero- or low-alcohol beverage or cutting out alcohol altogether—the choices for sober sipping no longer suck. Sure, plenty of places still omit the spirit to make a "virgin" cocktail without adjusting other ingredients, which throws off the balance of the original. In others, non-alcoholic options often end up being a Sophie's choice: cloying concoction or dull-as-dishwater diet soda. Skip those spots. The places you want to drink are ones where creativity doesn't disappear with the ABV. The beverages that follow are hardly afterthoughts playing a supporting part on the menu. In some cases, they might even steal some of the spotlight. No sober second thoughts required.

LAVANDA FIZZ

THE ACORN, RILEY PARK

Representing summer in Vancouver and a beverage enjoyed by all, the LaVANda Fizz is an aromatic, refreshing, citrusy, and sparkling non-alcoholic cocktail," says Shira Blustein of The Acorn, a vegetarian restaurant that uses seasonal ingredients at their peak. "We can find lavender growing pretty much everywhere around our neighborhood, and we grow it in our restaurant garden. We forage the sumac and dry it out along with the lavender so we can enjoy this mocktail all year round."

GLASSWARE: Collins glass
GARNISH: Lavender and Sumac Salt Rim (see recipe at right), lavender sprig

- 1½ oz. (45 ml) Lavender and Sumac Syrup (see recipe at right)
- 1 oz. (30 ml) lemon juice
- 4 oz. (120 ml) soda water
- 2 dashes Peychaud's bitters (optional*)

1. Garnish the rim of a collins glass with the Lavender and Sumac Salt Rim.

2. Add the Lavender and Sumac Syrup, lemon juice, and soda water. Stir.

3. Carefully fill the glass with ice. Add 2 dashes of Peychaud's bitters (optional*).

4. Garnish the cocktail with the fresh lavender sprig.

*Adding bitters is optional, imparting hints of spice to the cocktail. Although the recipe only calls for a couple of dashes, Peychaud's and other bitters and tinctures have an ABV of 35 to 44 percent.

LAVENDER AND SUMAC SYRUP: In a medium-size pot, add ½ cup (125 ml) dried lavender, ½ cup (125 ml) dried sumac, 2 cups (500 grams) organic cane sugar, and 2 cups (500 ml) water. Bring the mixture to a boil for 30 minutes. Let cool for another 30 minutes. Fine-strain the syrup into a sealable 1-liter container.

LAVENDER AND SUMAC SALT RIM: In a blender or spice grinder, blend 2¼ teaspoons (10 grams) each of salt, dried lavender, and dried sumac until you have a coarse grain that's well mixed.

JAMAIQUITA LEMONADE

CAFÉ MEDINA, DOWNTOWN

There's something slightly provocative about sitting at a bar staring at gleaming glass bottles during breakfast (especially when happy hour runs from 9 to 11 a.m.). And the one in Café Medina is like a magnet, pulling people to its metal stools for the city's best brunch. The café has always had a cult following for its Mediterranean-inspired dishes and its creative beverages—boozy or not. The Jamaiquita Lemonade is a great non-alcoholic option that's a hit for the early crowd. The recipe is a nod to the popular mint tea in Morocco.

GLASSWARE: Collins glass
GARNISH: Fresh mint sprig

- 1½ oz. (45 ml) Hibiscus Eucalyptus Syrup (see recipe at right)
- 1 oz. (30 ml) lemon juice
- Soda, to top
- 2 dashes grapefruit bitters

1. Add the Hibiscus Eucalyptus Syrup and lemon juice to the collins glass.

2. Top with ice and soda. Add the bitters.

3. Garnish with the mint sprig.

HIBISCUS EUCALYPTUS SYRUP: In a saucepan, combine 4¼ cups (1 liter) white sugar, 4¼ cups (1 liter) water, ¼ cup (34 grams) dried hibiscus, and 1 drop eucalyptus oil. Bring the mixture to a light boil. Simmer for 30 minutes. Let it cool. Strain the syrup into a bottle and store it in the refrigerator.

COMMERCIAL DRIVE

L'ABATTOIR RESTAURANT, GASTOWN

L'Abattoir bartenders Dave Bulters and Rob Williams came up with this low-ABV play on the espresso-and-tonic craze that spread across the globe some years ago. Named for the street in East Vancouver famous for its coffee-and-food culture, this bubbly cocktail is a low-ABV alternative to an Espresso Martini.

According to Bulters, the combination of coffee and Cynar was inspired by his mother-in-law. She often finishes a meal with an espresso and a side of the amaro. The tropical element brought in by the bitters was introduced by Williams, whose preferred serve for coffee has long been with fresh pineapple juice.

Curious about the alcohol content? Cynar comes in at 16.5 percent, while the Wayward Distillery Vodka lands at 33 percent ABV.

GLASSWARE: Collins glass
GARNISH: Lemon twist

- 1 oz. (30 ml) Wayward Distillery Depth Charge Espresso and Cacao Bean Vodka Infusion

- 1 oz. (30 ml) Cynar

- 1 oz. (30 ml) East Van Roasters Espresso

- 5 drops Ms. Better's Pineapple Star Anise Bitters

- Fever-Tree Indian Tonic, to top

1. Combine all of the ingredients, except the tonic, in a collins glass with ice.

2. Add the tonic and gently stir. Express the lemon oil from the twist over the drink and garnish with the twist.

MARGUERITE DAISY

Marc Smolinski, bar manager at Vij's, decided to reverse-engineer the Margarita to make a nonalcoholic version, starting with tasting notes for a good blanco tequila. "I get black agave, pepper, aloe, and spicy notes that tingle on the tongue." Next, he infused a BC-distilled nonalcoholic gin with black pepper and sansho peppers—"the sansho gives a prickly feeling on the tongue that mimics the burn from alcohol." Does it measure up to the original? Marc says, "A guest came up to the bar to double-check that his pregnant wife had not been served a real Margarita after they both tasted it and thought it had tequila in it." Mission accomplished.

◆

GLASSWARE: Old-fashioned glass
GARNISH: Salt rim, lime wedge

- 2 oz. (60 ml) Pepper-Infused Lumette! Light Alt-Spirit (see recipe at right)
- 1 oz. (30 ml) aloe juice
- 1 oz. (30 ml) lime juice
- ⅓ oz. (10 ml) orange juice
- ⅓ oz. (10 ml) agave syrup
- ⅓ oz. (10 ml) simple syrup

1. Pour all of the ingredients into a mixing tin.

2. Add ice; shake.

3. Salt half the rim of an old-fashioned glass. Strain the cocktail into the glass over ice.

4. Garnish with the lime wedge.

PEPPER-INFUSED LUMETTE! LIGHT ALT-SPIRIT: Using a funnel, add 1 teaspoon (5 ml) ground black pepper and 1 teaspoon (5 ml) ground sansho pepper to 25½ oz. (750 ml) nonalcoholic gin. Seal the bottle and let the gin infuse for 48 hours. Fine-strain before using.

THE VITALIZER

OLD BIRD, MOUNT PLEASANT

Bartender Phoebe Wilkinson grew up in Thailand, where tamarind trees were the norm, but when she came to Canada, she did not have the luxury of paradise at her fingertips. However, it was here that she saw and tasted grapefruit for the first time in her life. In The Vitalizer, Wilkinson combines these two flavors in one glass to remind her of this experience.

She says, "This used to be one of Old Bird's most popular zero-proof cocktails. It is savory and refreshing; this drink will revitalize you."

GLASSWARE: Coupe glass, chilled

GARNISH: Lime salt rim

- 1½ oz. (45 ml) Tamarind Syrup (see recipe at right)
- 1½ oz. (45 ml) grapefruit juice
- 1 oz. (30 ml) lime juice
- Pinch of Lime Salt (see recipe at right)
- 1 dash Ms. Better's Bitters Miraculous Foamer

1. Combine all of the ingredients in a cocktail shaker; add ice.

2. Shake hard for 30 seconds.

3. Rim the chilled coupe with the Lime Salt.

4. Double-strain the cocktail into the glass.

TAMARIND SYRUP: Combine equal parts tamarind concentrate and simple syrup. Mix well before each use. Store in the refrigerator.

LIME SALT: Dehydrate lime peels and grind them into powder. Mix equal part kosher and sea salt with lime powder.

WATERMELON CUCUMBER SODA

HAVANA, COMMERCIAL DRIVE

Necessity is often the mother of invention. One of Vancouver's hottest summers on record and an unexpected heatwave meant all hands on deck at Havana," says Alexa Greenman, beverage director. "This drink was born out of demand from Andrew Hounslow, Havana's executive chef. Working hours on end, Andrew would ask me for something that would keep him alive through our unending rushes."

Playing off flavors from Havana's authentic Latin-style food and local ingredients inspired her to bring that same energy into small but impactful drinks. "It ended up being a different drink every day," she says. "The last of dozens of creations was this drink. From then on, it became Andrew's go-to. I promised him that I'd put it on the menu and find a way to credit him for it. This is that exact opportunity."

GLASSWARE: Round-bottom collins glass
GARNISH: Cucumber ribbon, mint leaves

- 1 oz. (30 ml) lime juice
- 1 oz. (30 ml) Cucumber-Watermelon Juice (see recipe at right)
- ½ oz. (15 ml) orgeat
- 3 oz. (90 ml) soda water

1. Wrap the cucumber ribbon inside the collins glass. Add ice.

2. Add all of the fresh ingredients. Top with the soda water.

3. Garnish with fresh mint leaves.

CUCUMBER-WATERMELON JUICE: In a blender, combine half a peeled cucumber and one-third of a rindless watermelon cut into cubes. Add 2 cups (500 ml) of water and blend well. Double-strain the juice through a fine filter.

FAIRMONT WATERFRONT'S BEES KNEES

ARC BAR, FAIRMONT WATERFRONT, DOWNTOWN

This zero-proof take on the classic Bees Knees omits the usual gin but not the texture and taste of honey, which in this case is harvested from the hotel's rooftop apiary. And instead of juniper, this cocktail's aromatic and earthy elements come from rosemary grown in the third-floor terrace garden. It makes for a hyper-local sip, which is the foundation of ARC Bar's garden-to-glass cocktail menu, like the Flaming Rosemary Gimlet on page 51.

GLASSWARE: Rocks glass
GARNISH: Rosemary sprig or lemon wedge

- 1 oz. (30 ml) Rosemary-Honey Simple Syrup (see recipe at right)
- Half a lemon
- Sparkling water, to top

1. Add ice to a rocks glass (or small drinking glass) until three-quarters of the way full.

2. Add the syrup, and squeeze in the juice from the lemon half.

3. Top with sparkling water until the glass is full. Stir to combine.

4. Garnish with the rosemary sprig or lemon wedge.

ROSEMARY-HONEY SIMPLE SYRUP:
In a small saucepan, add 1 cup (250 ml) honey
and 1 cup (250 ml) water. Heat over medium
heat, stirring occasionally until the honey dissolves. Turn off the heat. Add one sprig of
rosemary. Cover and let the honey syrup steep
for 20 minutes. Remove and discard the rosemary. Strain the syrup into a glass jar and
store it in the refrigerator.

APPENDIX: HOW TO BUILD YOUR HOME BAR

Whether you call it art, science, or alchemy, creating a cocktail starts with stellar ingredients. Many drinks can be built right in the glass, like a Caesar or gin and tonic, but when a recipe calls for shaking, stirring, and muddling, bar tools are essential. You can spend thousands building your home bar with luxury items such as gold-plated cocktail shakers or ice ball makers (in aerospace-grade aluminum, no less), but it's easy to find good-quality and affordable tools that will last for years. Start with some basics, then add to the collection as you expand your experience.

EASY DRINKING (BEGINNER)

JIGGER

Skip the shot glass and get a jigger (or two). Often made of stainless steel, this V- or cup-shaped vessel typically holds 1 oz. Look for ones with etched lines inside for smaller quantities. Double-sided jiggers (shaped like an hourglass) often have 1 oz. and 2 oz. or ½ oz. and ¾ oz. capacities for versatility and precision measuring.

SHAKER

The two most common types are the cobbler and Boston shaker. Each has benefits and drawbacks, but any decent shaker will yield frothy whiskey sours and a perfectly chilled Paper Plane.

Cobbler

This classic three-part shaker has a built-in strainer and a cap that often doubles as a 1 oz. measure. Sleek lines and mirrored or brushed-metal finishes make cobblers eye-catching choices for  the home bar, but they can be leaky, difficult to pry open, and the strainer has a slow pour. That might seem trivial, but these smaller shakers only hold a single cocktail, so they can be impractical for entertaining.

Boston Shaker

This bartender stalwart is composed of a weighted shaking tin and a mixing glass (a pint glass does the trick) or two tins of different sizes. Ingredients and ice go in the large tin, and the glass or smaller tin is inverted on top to make an airtight seal (give it a solid slap to open). The typical stainless steel Boston shaker isn't nearly as sexy or sophisticated-looking as the cobbler, but matte black and copper- or gold-plated tins are starting to snag some spotlight.

TIN VS. GLASS

You see the phrases "tin on glass" or "tin on tin," but this bartender preference doesn't hold as much weight in home bars. Glass lets you see what you're mixing, but it can chip or break if you're not careful. Two tins maintain a more consistent temperature when shaking. There are various tin sizes; larger ones have more room for ice and aeration, ideal for creating cocktails with egg whites or vegan foamer. Another upside to tin on tin: you can make two cocktails at once.

HAWTHORNE STRAINER

The Boston shaker's best friend is the Haw-thorne strainer. Composed of a perforated metal flat plate, with two to four flat prongs (or "ears"), its signature wire coils fit tightly inside the tin or glass, keeping ice and herbs out of your cocktail.

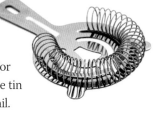

CITRUS JUICER

A handheld wooden reamer, metal clamp-like squeezer, or countertop press (with a recepta-cle for catching liquid and a spout for pouring) are all affordable tools for manually juicing lemons and limes. You still need to watch out for seeds, pulp, and pith; some countertop presses have handy strainers.

CRUSH AND SQUEEZE

A heavy-duty countertop citrus press is a great investment for juicing larger citrus such as grape-fruit and oranges, as well as crushing apples, pome-granate, and pineapple. These manual machines are often made of cast iron and have a powerful arm lever for quickly pressing large quantities of fruit.

ICE BUCKET AND TONGS

Don't overlook this essential item, especially when hosting a party. Bagged ice might be handy, but you don't want guests groping around in the freezer to find it or fussing with ice trays. Look for an ice bucket with double-walled insulation and a fitted lid.

SOPHISTICATED SIPPING (INTERMEDIATE)

MIXING GLASS

Sure, you can stir a Manhattan in a shaker tin or pint glass with a tapered bottom, but buying a bigger vessel with a broad base is worth the investment (less than a bottle of whiskey). A go-to is Japanese brand Yarai (often used as a catchall word for other brands), which manufactures thick-walled, cylindrical in various capacities (17 oz. to 23 oz.) glasses that hold lots of ice and liquid when making multiple cocktails.

FORM AND FUNCTION

The weight of the glass and absence of a seam on the inside allow for smooth stirring to combine, chill, and dilute the ingredients with ice while maintaining the cocktail's clarity and texture. Mixing glasses have a spout for splash-free pouring.

BARSPOON

Using a barspoon with a long, spindly spiral handle might seem pretentious, but it's actually a fine-tuned tool. Along with its self-evident use for measuring ingredients and stirring cocktails, some barspoons come with trident tips for fishing garnishes like onions, olives, and cherries from jars. Others feature flat or disc-shaped ends for muddling. So, what's with the spiral? It's for layering liquor; slowly pour alcohol down the handle to create a smooth flow. You can also use the bowl or back of the spoon to create layered cocktails like the New York Sour on page 125.

JULEP STRAINER

A julep strainer, which looks like a large metal spoon with small holes in it, goes hand in hand with stirred drinks to strain out ice. In many respects, introduction of the Hawthorne strainer usurped its importance. The julep strainer was invented for drinking (not making) cocktails to keep crushed ice off sensitive teeth and out of men's beards. It's still a fully functional traditional tool and statement piece to elevate your home bar. Plus a julep's smooth surface is easier to clean than a Hawthorne's coils.

MUDDLER

If you plan to make mojitos, mules, or the Lulumelon (see page 320), a proper muddler is a must. The bartender's analog to the pestle, this cylindrical tool is used to gently break down fruit and aromatics and extract juice and oils from citrus.

BUYING TIPS

Muddlers come in materials from metal and solid wood to stone and food-grade silicon. Some have grooves on the "head" that are great for getting oils out of citrus. Overaggressive muddling with these can bruise delicate herbs like basil. Instead, consider a muddler with a rounded head.

CHANNEL KNIFE

The easiest way to make a pro-looking lemon twist is with a channel knife. It's an affordable tool that lets you strip off citrus peel in thin strips without worrying about taking off too much pith, which can add bitterness to your drink. Kitchen stores often carry a two-in-one tool that has a rasp for zesting citrus at the top and a channel knife along the side.

KING CUBE ICE TRAY

King Cube is one brand of silicon mold for making extra-large square ice cubes, but there are plenty of food-grade trays to be found. Not only do big hunks of ice look stunning in cocktails like an Old Fashioned, they melt slower, keeping your drink chilled without diluting it too quickly.

NEXT-LEVEL IMBIBING (ADVANCED)

FINE-MESH STRAINER

Small, round and with a deep scoop, use this basic tool in tandem with a Hawthorne to double-strain cocktails, filtering out even the smallest flecks of mint or shards of ice. Hold the fine-mesh strainer in one hand over the glass and use the other hand to pour.

LEWIS BAG

If you want to make the Rickshaw (see page 182) but don't have a blender with a crushed-ice setting, go old school and buy a Lewis bag. It's a rectangular sack made of professional-grade canvas you fill with cubes, then crush with a wooden mallet.

COCKTAIL SMOKER

Cocktail smokers, which are basically a butane torch and food-grade wood chips, are surprisingly simple and affordable for home use. It's more about science than style, though the theater of it is pretty impressive. Smoke imparts a complexity to a cocktail by interacting with its components and infusing fruity or savory essences to the spirits. Test it out by making the Published Martini No. 5 (see page 226).

MISTER OR ATOMIZER

A mister works in the same way as spritzing orange zest over a cocktail (and rim of the glass) to add a hit of aroma, without actually adding the element to a drink's ingredients. For instance, a mist vermouth over a dry martini or absinthe over a Sazerac.

STOCK THE BAR: FINDING TOOLS OF THE TRADE IN VANCOUVER

MODERN BARTENDER

For more than a decade, Modern Bartender has kept locals stocked with tools for shaking, stirring, straining, smoking, and garnishing cocktails. Located in Chinatown, Modern Bartender also stocks a selection of bitters and syrups, many made locally, and drinkware and cocktail books galore.

ATKINSON'S

This high-end boutique in South Granville sells an impressive selection of bar tools. You can find everything from bitters bottles and shakers crafted from French crystal to champagne sabers. Japanese and European brands are prominently featured.

THE GOURMET WAREHOUSE

Chef, author, and TV personality Caren McSherry is the owner and powerhouse behind this housewares and food mecca that's been in operation since 1998. The sprawling store on East Hastings Street downtown carries bar tools such as jiggers, mixing glasses, and citrus presses, plus paper straws and cocktail picks.

ACKNOWLEDGMENTS

First, I would like to acknowledge that the lands where I have the privilege to live and work are situated on the unceded traditional territories of the xʷməθkʷəy̓əm (Musqueam), S̱ḵwx̱wú7mesh (Squamish), and səlilwətal (Tsleil-Waututh) Nations.

I am so grateful to be surrounded by a community of family, friends, writers, editors, and publishers, among others who have supported me and my work over the years. None of it would have been possible without you, Dad. Thank you for teaching me to work hard, dream big, and for being my champion as I've zigged and zagged through this thing called life.

To my sister, Sue, I don't say it nearly enough, but thank you for . . . everything. That includes your rapid replies to my random, "Can you read this?!" texts and keeping me well-versed in puns and *Seinfeld* lore. To Dave, you're the best "bro." I deeply respect your sage advice, and thank you for fueling me with breakfast sandwiches and coffee when needed. And to Zach, my love, what an adventure we've been on, from desert to sea and whatever is yet to come. Your unflagging support, especially with this book, is everything. Thank you for your generous spirit and always being game to join me on writing recon missions even in the middle of nowhere.

I have the smartest, funniest, most badass group of friends who always have my back and a kind word—when I let them get one in edgewise. Thank you, Christina Newberry, my friend and fellow writer, for paying it forward. I love how our story started on that tiny sturgeon-fishing boat and morphed into exploring cool places on three continents. What will we get up to next?

A super-loud shoutout to Melissa Harder. I think (know) your excitement for this book matched mine. Thank you for being the best cocktail-sipping partner and a bright light on dark days. You know I'll never take a taxi to Brazil with anyone else. My appreciation and admiration goes to Charlene Rooke, another writer who knows her way around the world of booze. Girl, you're a great friend and make a mean cocktail. Thank you for contributing your expertise to this book.

Massive thanks, of course, go to the team at Cider Mill Press and HarperCollins Focus, especially editors Buzz Poole and Jeremy E. Hauck. Your trust in inviting me to write this book, and giving me the creative freedom to shape it, is a writer's dream.

Naturally, *Vancouver Cocktails* could only exist with the collective efforts of the city's bartenders, restaurateurs, and crew who contributed their favorite recipes, techniques, and tips. I can't thank you enough for your generosity in sharing your inspiration and stories behind the cocktails. My mind was constantly blown by the creativity being cultivated in this city.

To write this book, I interviewed a number experts about booze who educated me about the industry they're so deeply committed to. Sincere thanks to Leagh Barkley, Alex Black, Alex Hamer, Trevor Kallies, and Charlene Rooke. I couldn't have pulled everything together without the assistance of Vancouver's stellar PR pros and their teams who put me in touch with people, and wrangled recipes and photos: Tara Armstrong, Gemma Bishop, Allie Darwin, Ksenia Dempster, Paul Done, Kelly Jordan Hamilton, Michelle Lam, Katharine Manson, Shelley McArthur Everett, Laura Serena, Morgan Sommerville, Kaylyn Storey, and an extra-special thanks to Sophia Cheng for going above and beyond.

ABOUT THE AUTHOR

Janet Gyenes is an award-winning writer, photographer, and editor whose wanderlust has taken her to almost forty countries. Where she travels, Janet likes to learn what locals are distilling and brewing. She's sipped bush beer on the island of Atiu in the South Pacific, biked to wineries in Mendoza, drank homemade snake wine in Vietnam, and sipped baijiu while horse-trekking in Inner Mongolia. A former beverage columnist for a lifestyle magazine, Janet has been writing about beverages for more than a decade. Several of her articles have received awards from the North American Travel Journalist Association (NATJA) in the culinary journalism category.

Janet grew up on the Sunshine Coast of British Columbia but has lived in Vancouver for most of her life. She spent three years in China, where she explored Shanghai's stellar bar scene. She is the co-author of two books, *Moon Metro Vancouver* and *Vancouver: The Complete Residents' Guide*, and her work has appeared in *Lonely Planet*, *Smithsonian*, Culture Trip, and *USA Today*. Janet is an avid photographer, and she enjoys exploring the city by bike, hiking the forest trails, and getting out on the water whenever possible.

PHOTOGRAPHY CREDITS

Pages 27, 70, 73, 210 by Mark Yammine; pages 37, 235 by Eric Milic Photography; page 42 by Leila Kwok; pages 47, 319 by Clinton Hussey; pages 55, 57 by Jonathan Thompson; page 65 by Ryan Guthrie; pages 77, 285 by Kyle Humeny; pages 91, 203, 204, 252 by Viranlly Liemena; pages 97, 99, 101, 103, 329, 345 by Ksenia Dempster; pages 106–07, 111, 277 by Natahsha Priya; pages 113, 114, 267 by Katie Huisman; pages 79, 123, 124, 127, 150–51, 173, 176, 231, 232 by Juno Kim; pages 130, 275 by Mia Glanz; pages 132, 135, 136, 245 by Simon Brown; page 139 by Sierra Webb; page 141 by Denton Meyer; page 145 by Andrew King and Tarquin Melnyk; pages 147–149 by Mark Yammine, et al; page 159 by Hakan Burcuoglu; pages 165, 167 by Katie Jameson; pages 169, 335 by Lorenzo Ignacio; pages 175, 236, 240 by Chelsea Brown; pages 179, 181 by Breanne Smart; pages 183, 313 by Coulter Noronha; page 185 by RD Cane; page 187 by Glowbal Group; page 192 by Janet Gyenes; pages 198, 283, 288 by Josh Neufeld Photography; page 207 by Will Luk; page 209 by Angel Lynne; pages 214–15, 339 by Dave Bulters; pages 225, 227, 229, 258, 261, 298–99 by Sarah Annand; page 243 by Cody Chan; page 255 by Sebastian Fuertes; page 272 by SMC Communications; page 291 by Gabrielle Lee; pages 303, 305 by Allison Kuhl; page 306 by Joel Boh; page 321 by Brandon Meyer.

Pages 1, 3, 4–5, 6, 28–29, 66–67, 80, 188–89, 246–47, 278–79, 330–31, 348–57 used under official license from Shutterstock.com.

Pages 10, 17 courtesy of Vancouver Public Library.

Pages 11, 15 courtesy of the City of Vancouver Archives.

Pages 12, 16, 19, 21 courtesy of Library of Congress.

Page 22 courtesy of New York Public Library.

All other images courtesy of the respective bars and restaurants.

INDEX

—ABOUT CIDER MILL PRESS BOOK PUBLISHERS—

Good ideas ripen with time. From seed to harvest, Cider Mill Press brings fine reading, information, and entertainment together between the covers of its creatively crafted books. Our Cider Mill bears fruit twice a year, publishing a new crop of titles each spring and fall.

"Where Good Books Are Ready for Press"
501 Nelson Place
Nashville, Tennessee 37214
cidermillpress.com

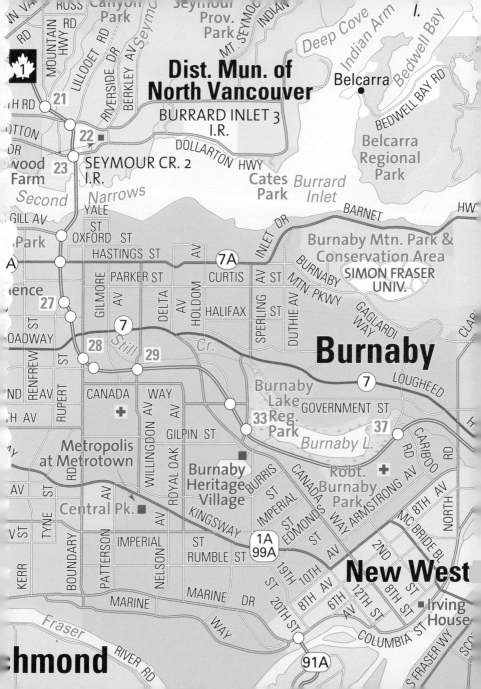